ISBN: 0999428608⌐SEP⌐
ISBN 13: 9780999428603⌐SEP⌐
Library of Congress Control Number: TXu 2-082-080
PBM Publications. Atlanta, GA

Police Brutality Matters is dedicated to Sandra Bland (July 13, 2015), Philando Castile (July 6, 2016), Eric Garner (July 17, 2014), Jordan Edwards (April 29, 2017), Walter Scott (April 4, 2015), Freddie Gray (April 19, 2015), Alton B. Sterling (July 5, 2016), Oscar Grant III (January 1, 2009), Tamir Rice (November 22, 2014), Laquan McDonald (October 20, 2014), Samuel Dubose (July 19, 2015), Sean Bell (November 25, 2006), Terence Crutcher (September 16, 2016), Akai Gurley (November 20, 2014), Aiyana Jones (May 16, 2010), Korryn Gaines (August 2, 2016), Amadou Diallo (February 4, 1999)

CONTENTS

Chapter 1   The Culture of Policing   1

Chapter 2   The Negative Black Subculture   19

Chapter 3   Discretion or Discrimination   30

Chapter 4   Protect Us or Police Them   49

Chapter 5   Racism within the Blue Walls   73

Chapter 6   The Cover-Up   86

Chapter 7   Tricks of the Trade   120

             The U.S. Constitution   145

             About the Author   152

             Acknowledgement   153

             Endnotes/Credits   154

             Glossary   156

Police Brutality Matters

CHAPTER ONE

The Culture of Policing

American policing has unique characteristics that distinguish it from other occupations such as having the power to kill, taking someone's liberty and freedom, being authorized to strip someone of his or her constitutional rights, and investigating itself. As an essential part of American society, policing shared many characteristics and concerns with white America during and following the end of slavery. The legal system of the United States and the norms it created conformed to white American standards during that period. Law enforcement incorporated behaviors, viewed as entirely appropriate by white Americans that routinely violated the rights of blacks and minorities. For example, though in 1870, the Fifteenth Amendment of the U.S. Constitution was passed, section 1 stating, "The right of citizens of the United States to vote shall not be denied or abridged by the United States or any State because of race, color, or previous condition of servitude." As early as 1865, legislatures in Confederate states enacted "black codes." These codes prohibited blacks from renting land, traveling, learning to read, the right to bear arms, and the right to assemble except for religious purposes, just to name a few. Many blacks were bogusly charged and arrested for various infractions, and they were forced to serve as free laborers for white owners of businesses, including plantations.

Policing was established due to the mob violence and racial indifference of slavery. During this period, slave patrols were charged with recapturing escaped slaves. Following the end of slavery, an era of widespread violence against newly freed slaves and immigrants began; they adapted and learned to deal with the racial conflict that was now a daily fact of life. As the newly freed slaves and the immigrant population grew across the country, it became extremely difficult to organize mob groups to instill fear and commit violent acts. White Americans began to realize that a more structured process was needed to control these groups of people. Before the end of slavery, police departments were created. Boston created the first police department in 1838, followed by New York in 1844 and Philadelphia in 1854. These so-called police departments inherited the functions of the mobs they replaced.

The experience of becoming a police officer and the history of policing itself caused many officers to band together in what is known as the *"blue wall of silence."* Officers tend to stand together and cut off all others who are not considered law enforcement. Joining a police department is like taking an oath to that blue wall. Members of this type of subculture, as with any other gang, are taught to stick up for each other against all others. They are loyal to fellow cops above all, and everyone else is secondary. They'll do whatever it takes, even if it means bending the rules. They express many sentiments such as these: "Criminals, people of color, and nonwhite immigrants have too many civil rights, and we need to do whatever is necessary to control them all. The public is unsupportive, and people only like us when they need something. Forget that bullshit they teach you in the academy about helping people and fighting crime."

The chronology of how this country was founded, policing was established, and slaves were freed supports the negative values and attitudes about minorities held by police officers, which causes secrecy and isolation from the rest of society. This has produced a gang culture in the criminal justice system. We, the people in policing, feel the need to use force and authority over others to control them. If you do not comply, you are subject to physical or even *deadly force*. The *police culture* teaches officers that blacks and minorities are potentially violent and likely to commit crimes due to the history of slavery. Blacks in America are more likely to come from deteriorated neighborhoods and have economic disadvantages, while foreigners are coming to America from third-world countries. Many blacks had to endure poor living conditions during and after slavery. Housed on plantations, most slaves lived in one-room shacks that were in extremely poor condition. Imagine living in a place where the roof leaks; there are holes in the walls; the chimney is clogged, providing poor ventilation and routinely causing fires; and there are unfinished dirt floors and open drafts throughout. Many slaves died from numerous diseases, while others sustained permanent physical and psychological damage.

The behaviors that support this *police culture* are developed from *street training* and on-the-job experiences passed down from the senior officers. The historical socialization and prior practices of police forces cause these character traits to develop in police officers. In the academy, police officers are taught to bond with fellow officers while learning the proper legal procedures. It is from seasoned police officers that the rookies learn how to follow the law when applicable or ignore departmental rules and regulations while using personal discretion to their advantage. Many individuals become police officers because they want to help people and fight crime. Once they become members of the police force, they develop a unique set of police cultural traits that are distinct from those of a normal society. This police-culture personality is typically authoritarian, racist, hostile, suspicious, cynical, and dogmatic. It is these gang-like negative values and attitudes that police officers develop subconsciously against blacks, Latinos, and other minorities.

An important part of police social structure is the development of factious or gang-like groups. There is a culture of violence in policing, encouraging its members to engage in senseless brutality. They become prone to such violence because this behavior is the norm of the organization. Notice the characteristics of a gang in comparison to the various groups such as Bloods and Crips, Hells Angels, and MS-13. "Gang" is a term widely used in society to refer to groups such as motorcycle/bike gangs, prison gangs, street gangs, organized crime, hate groups, terrorist groups, and other types of threat organizations.

The text below describes a gang in *Italic* lettering and the structure of law enforcement in **bold**; notice the similarities.

The definition of a gang is as follows:
An association of three or more individuals (**such as departments, divisions, units, or platoons**) *whose members collectively identify themselves by adopting a group identity, which they use to create an atmosphere of fear or intimidation, frequently by employing one or more of the following:*

a common name, slogan, identifying sign, symbol, tattoo or other physical marking, style or color of clothing, hairstyle, hand sign or graffiti (**as in police, sheriff, cop, and so on, "to protect and serve," the symbol of the badge or police car, uniforms, color of clothing, and hand signs**), [and] whose purpose in part is to engage in criminal activity with the intent to enhance or preserve the association's power, reputation, or economic resources. (**Power and control, uses intimidation and violence to further its objectives of gaining compliance, and has authoritative behavior with a focus on generating revenue.**)

The association may also possess some of the following characteristics:

The members may employ rules for joining and operating within the association. (**Police officers take an oath and use a standard operational procedure manual.**) The members may meet on a recurring basis at various locations. (**Law enforcement employs many methods to transmit and disseminate information, such as roll call, unit and division meetings, and other debriefings such as comp stat.**) Gang associations will provide physical protection of their members from others. (**Police officers use unnecessary physical force, *excessive force*, and even *deadly force* to those who fail to comply with an unlawful arrest.**) The association may seek to exercise control over a geographic *territory, location, or region, or may simply defend its perceived interests against rivals.* (**Law enforcement has numerous jurisdictions, such as federal, state, local, city, county, town, and village, with geographical boundaries throughout the country.**) *The association may have an identifiable structure such as a leader, captain, lieutenant, soldier, enforcer, and so on.* (**Police organizational charts will often include a chain of command, including rank and file with titles like chief or commissioner, deputy chief, major, captain, lieutenant, sergeant, detective, and officer.**) Both groups have an *unwritten code* about providing information to investigating authorities relating to their conduct and activities. *The gang's code of honor is to not snitch on each other,* whereas **police officers use the same code of honor not to rat each other out**.

There is no single explanation as to why various forms of abuse occur in policing. One explanation puts the blame on the historical relationship between the police and minorities. Blacks were considered only property to slave owners, and immigrants were looked upon as a competitive threat to the working and lower-class citizens. The opportunities in policing tend to attract those from all walks of life, particularly special interest groups that are extremely cohesive and powerful and those who feel the white race as being superior over all races. They can promote their beliefs using the criminal justice system. They support a political, economic, and cultural system that perpetuates and maintains their ideology.

Infiltrating law enforcement allows these individuals to commit violent acts against others with very little to no legal ramifications. With the support of the courts and government, civil and criminal repercussions are of no concern. Many of these subjects come from militia groups with extremist views. They are well educated and operate in a hidden fashion, speaking and dressing normally and using no racial epithets in their normal dialogue. Because violence and abuse are a function of police institutions and practices, many members of other nonwhite ethnic groups join law enforcement and conform to the violent culture. They abuse others while seeking approval from those within the organization. Similarly, police supervisors and managers alike have risen through the ranks and are reluctant to investigate such abuse or punish wrongdoers.

Here's the million-dollar question: How can *excessive force* and abuse by police be controlled? One approach is to use state-of-the-art technology, such as the most sophisticated video- and audio-recording equipment, along with a more stringent psychological evaluation. There should be a strong external investigating agency outside of the police department, an accountable internal administrative review unit, and a strong internal affairs division, and civil rights violations specifically for law enforcement should be established and defined. Legislatures need to pass and enforce laws governing these criminal justice procedures. The government needs to give law enforcement and all other agencies within the criminal justice system a strong and fair warning of the nature of forbidden conduct and describe in detail the sanctions associated with such criminal behavior. Following this, well-publicized punishments connected to those employed in the criminal justice system will serve to deter other members from carrying out illegal acts. If punishment is severe and if criminal justice employees believe they are likely to be caught, the threat of such accountability should be sufficient to deter their behavior.

Finally, there should be a reconstruction of the courts system involving the prosecutors and the grand jury process. The prosecutor is responsible for bringing the state's case against individuals who disobey the law within their jurisdiction. Subjects can be charged with a crime, excused from prosecution, or brought to trial. The prosecutor's primary duty should be to enforce criminal law with a fundamental obligation to seek justice for all by convicting those who are guilty. The prosecutor has the responsibility of proving to an objective group of citizens that there is probable cause to believe that a crime was committed, and that the accused should be tried regarding the matter. This process is ordinarily known as an indictment resulting from a grand jury hearing. An indictment is written by a prosecutor charging a person or people with a crime, and it is then submitted to a grand jury. After hearing all the evidence presented by the prosecutor, the grand jury votes to endorse (true bill) or deny (no true bill) the indictment. A prosecutor has a wide range of discretion in decisions to charge a subject with a crime.

The prosecutor and the police have a very important relationship. The prosecutor heavily relies on law enforcement officers to provide and initiate formal complaints against individuals. In most cases, the prosecutor maintains regular contact with police officers to develop the criminal prosecution systematically and efficiently. Because of the close ties to law enforcement and political influences, many prosecutors weaken the effectiveness of the prosecutorial process in investigating and prosecuting criminal offenses related to police officers. Prosecutors have been criticized due to their broad discretion and their lack of effort to secure indictments when presenting a fair and unbiased case against police officials.

Cases that go before a grand jury take significantly longer than ordinary citizens' cases. This process is inefficient and needs great improvement, since the prosecution can steer the hearing in the direction of its desired outcome. The grand jury is empowered to act as an independent investigative body. The investigative efforts are once again controlled by the prosecution. After the investigation is completed, a presentment is issued. The presentment contains information concerning the findings of the grand jury, along with a recommendation of indictment. This same grand jury relies on the testimony of witnesses called by the prosecution. After examining the evidence and the testimony of witnesses, the grand jury decides whether probable cause exists for an indictment. What do you think the results will be if a prosecutor submits evidence that was collected and submitted at the crime scene by the police? What do you think the results will be if the prosecutor uses witness testimony that he determined was untruthful with many discrepancies? A grand jury ordinarily consists of sixteen to twenty-three citizens representing the county or jurisdiction in which they reside. Grand juries usually meet at the request of the prosecution. The prosecuting attorney presents evidence, calls witnesses, and makes a strong argument to obtain an indictment. A prosecutor can manipulate that process by presenting a weak case in special circumstances, such as police-related matters. Usually, the accused individuals are not allowed to attend the hearings, which are closed and secret. The effectiveness and efficiency of the grand jury procedure have been questioned for a few reasons following several police related deaths of **unarmed** black males.

The political process plays a significant role in shaping the various parts of the criminal justice system. Elected officials such as presidents, governors, mayors, prosecutors, sheriffs, and so on, normally have party affiliations with constituencies of voters and supporters. They tend to listen to their constituents and respond to community pressures and interests' groups' needs and demands. However, all elected officials must recognize that there should be no political favoritism or partisan bias in the enforcement of the law is applicable.

When it comes to elected officials and law enforcement, there should be no friends or enemies, just neutral standards and procedures that have the general public's best interests at heart. Elected officials should be people who have earned a reputation as trustworthy, professional, and unbiased. For example, the mayor of the City of New York oversees the executive branch of the city government. The mayor is a representative of all the people of New York City, not just one agency. If the citizens of New York City feel that there is any injustice or excessive use of force from the police, it is the mayor's job to acknowledge and correct the injustice. If that means making a correction to the policies and procedures of the police, that's his job. The mayor has acknowledged the rights of all New Yorkers to protest peacefully and demand police reform. He should not be blamed or apologize for allowing demonstrators to protest abusive and excessively aggressive police officers. A huge challenge for newly elected city mayors is to implement their policies governing law enforcement. It is especially a difficult task when dealing with agencies that have labor unions. Police unions across the country continue to have a significant impact on departmental administrations and policy decisions. Unions fight for increased salaries, improved benefits, and better departmental policies, including safety and operations affecting law enforcement. The union president is a key voice on labor-related policies that directly affect police officers. They meet with elected city officials to inform and assist them with what is needed to fight crime throughout communities while protecting all citizens.

Following the nationally publicized deaths of several unarmed black males who were killed at the hands of police, outcries for justice through protests and demonstrations in New York City and other cities across the country began to surface. A recording captured New York Police Department (NYPD) officers violently taking a man to the ground in the borough of Staten Island on July 17, 2014. The video shows a white male officer putting a large black man in a prohibited *chokehold* and taking him down to the ground with the assistance of approximately five to six other officers. The recording also shows the subject telling the police that he can't breathe. Prior to the prohibited *chokehold* by the police, the man, Eric Garner, was passively not cooperating as officers tried to place his hands in restraints. During this time, the man was complaining in a nonaggressive tone of voice about the ongoing harassment by the police, including prior contacts. After being choked to the ground and informing the officers that he couldn't breathe, seconds later, Mr. Garner was unconscious and unresponsive. Medical assistance was dispatched to the scene. The victim shortly thereafter went into cardiac arrest. While Emergency Medical Technicians (EMT) and paramedics attended to the victim, they appeared to be unconcerned with his condition. The video recording shows their lackadaisical commitment to his well-being. The video went viral, and millions of Americans and others across the world saw the *chokehold* incident. The mayor, who was on vacation out of the country at the time of the incident, commented on what he clearly viewed as a *chokehold*. The police commissioner also said that it appeared to be a *chokehold*. The American people were disbelieving and shocked by this video, and a united movement against police brutality began to surge even more strongly.

The head of the Police Benevolent Association (PBA), the NYPD's union for police officers, began addressing the *chokehold* incident with the media. The union president downplayed the incident, saying it was not a *chokehold* and implying that the incident was the victim's fault for resisting arrest. These comments outraged the public, creating a climate of tension between the police, government officials, and the public at large. The demands for justice and police reform and the shouts of protests intensified because of the police union president's circular logic. The demonstrations that have followed are protests police brutality and abusive practices, *excessive force*, violence, the *stop-and-frisk* of innocent citizens, lack of accountability and independent oversight, and more. What citizen would want this kind of police officer? Who would support police officers who would discriminate against any of their citizens and use excessive and *deadly force* unjustifiably? The mayor had acknowledged the people's right to peacefully protest and condemned the extremely small group of protesters who at any time chanted repulsive slogans against the police. After the release of the video from major media networks along with the mayor's comments, protests began to surface all around the country. The mayor was being accused of supporting an anti-police movement. Police union leaders also made the accusation that anti-police protests were the cause of the execution style slayings of two New York City police officers on December 20, 2014.

The protests gained momentum following a grand jury's decision not to indict the cop who had put Eric Garner in a prohibited *chokehold*. Following the incident, attention was paid to the wording used by police unions relating to anti-police versus anti-police brutality that was being projected at the mayor, politicians, the public, and anyone else who spoke against police injustice. Notice the demographic profile of those in opposition to certain law enforcement practices in contrast to its supporters. Many of the protesters were from various minority groups, including members of the LGBT community, labor unions, biracial and interracial groups, immigrant groups, organizations for women, and many other groups that support people of color. How about the media outlets that are affiliated with political parties? Numerous newspaper articles and certain affiliates of the media continuously mentioned that the president, attorney general, mayor of New York, and civil forces were waging an attack against the police. The crowds at pro-cop rallies and the neo Nazis and white supremacist followers that gather in support of Confederate flags and monuments are both supported by President Donald Trump. One rally was organized by a former NYPD captain with the support of a women's Republican group. Many pro-police supporters are active and retired police personnel, their family members, and numerous Republicans and their special interest groups such as the National Rifle Association (NRA), as well as others. While anti-police brutality rallies make it clear why they are protesting, pro-police groups are letting it be known that they support all police officers regardless of their behavior. Anti-police brutality organizers realize the importance of well-structured professional police departments within their communities across the country. They understand that policing is a vital institution in our society that maintains order in our communities, enforces laws, and responds to emergencies. There is a major concern regarding policing and the role the criminal justice system plays in controlling the behavior of law enforcement and protecting the public. Equal protection under the law can only be effective in the criminal justice system if we hold police accountable and ensure due process for all. Police departments across the country have the reputation that they are brutal and physically violent organizations. Historically, police officers resorted to violence and intimidation to gain respect from citizens through fear. The lack of accountability through the court system only exacerbates the conduct of the police.

Excessive force and police brutality have once again become the hot issue for government because of the constant video recordings and television coverage capturing police violence against Americans across the country. Today, police brutality and *deadly force* have become a great concern, particularly when police use *excessive force* against members of poor minority communities. Crime and police interactions will be higher in those areas, but the police behavior is not justified. The nation looked on in disgust when video footage was aired on network newscasts showing several recorded incidences involving police brutality.

On July 17, 2014, a recording captured an NYPD officer violently choking Eric Garner to the ground, using a *chokehold* that is prohibited by the department. *Chokehold*s are known to cut off the circulation of blood to the brain and can cause permanent damage or even death. On September 4, 2014, dash-cam video footage captured a South Carolina trooper shooting an unarmed motorist in the parking lot of a gas station. The trooper, Sean Groubert, stopped Levar Jones for a seatbelt violation. After the trooper asked for his license, Mr. Jones turned back toward his vehicle and reached inside to retrieve it. The trooper suddenly began shooting and yelling at Mr. Jones to get out of the car. Mr. Jones, who was hit in the hip with a bullet, could be heard on video saying, "I got my license. You said get my license."

On April 4, 2015, a cellular phone recording captured a police officer from North Charleston, South Carolina, shooting an unarmed man in the back while he was attempting to run away from the officer. The officer, Michael T. Slager, said he was in fear for his life because the man, identified as Walter Scott, had taken his stun gun in a scuffle following a traffic stop. The video, however, showed the officer firing his service weapon eight times as Mr. Scott fled. Mr. Scott appeared to have been fifteen to twenty feet away when fleeing. He then suddenly fell to the ground. Moments later, the officer ran back to where the initial scuffle occurred and picked something up off the ground. He then dropped an object that was later identified as a stun gun near Mr. Scott's body.

On November 26, 2015, a Cleveland police officer responded to a 911 call involving an armed subject pointing a pistol at individuals in a park at a nearby gazebo. The caller advised the communications dispatcher that the gun was probably fake and that the subject was probably a juvenile. The caller stated that the subject was scaring people. Then the caller left the park. The information provided by the caller was never relayed to the responding officers. Upon arriving at the park, Cleveland police officer Timothy Loehmann jumped out of the cruiser from the passenger side and, within two seconds, shot and killed a twelve-year-old boy later identified as Tamir Rice. It turned out that the twelve-year-old was in possession of a BB gun.

The *use of force* against these individuals and other minority citizens was the spark that set off nationwide protests and riots against excessive and brutal police behavior. Widely publicized incidents of police brutality have continued to emerge from police departments across the country. Why would any group of citizens rally behind police officers who behave as such? A special division that is responsible for enforcing laws and protecting the rights of individuals in the United States is needed urgently. A special department within the Department of Justice's (DOJ) civil rights division needs to be created to enforce laws that protect people from abuse by law enforcement agencies involving violations of federal civil rights laws. All citizens need to be protected from all discrimination based on their race, religion, creed, ethnicity, sexual preference, age, and gender.

Throughout the 1990's, a sudden shift that required police recruits to have a college education dramatically changed the personality within law enforcement. Most police departments in the United States now require recruits to have a college education. There is no evidence that college educated police officers perform better than less educated officers. The research is needed to determine whether such a shift in policing is beneficial or should immediately be reversed. Many qualified candidates, especially those from minority communities and whites who reside in diverse areas, are kept from opportunities in law enforcement because college degrees are required. I am confident that if a study were done on the value of police education versus police productivity, it would indicate that a college education does not influence police performance. The police role is diverse: it requires the ability to engage in dangerous situations, split second decision making, the ability to deescalate any situation at any given time, cultural diversity, and a high arrest to conviction rate. These are all things that a formal education for police officers cannot produce. Some police officers with college degrees do possess certain skills that are helpful in policing. For example, they are better report writers, using proper grammar, sentence structure, punctuation, and vocabulary. The educated officers tend to speak well during training seminars, conferences, and other areas where public speaking and formal verbal communication settings are used. These officers are very tech savvy, using charts, graphs, PowerPoint, and other computer software in their presentations. It should be recognized that an educational model centered around officers' ability to perform their jobs proficiently and professionally will be most effective for training current police officers. The model should not be centered on an unrelated academic program that is not essential to the officer's day-to- day duties. The ability to process and assess levels of danger quickly while initiating the proper *use of force* is what should be used to determine an officer's ability to react appropriately.

A police officer has the authority to use *deadly force* to kill suspects if they resist arrest while presenting imminent danger to the officer or others. Police officers are trained to use other proper methods of escalating force in response to the threats they face. Police officers are trained to assess the suspect's behavior and apply the appropriate or minimal amount of force needed to arrest or control a subject. *Deadly force* should be used only as a last resort. This type of reactive response is not one that can be measured through academics but is vital in an officer's daily functions. A simple analogy is how a sports commentator or broadcaster has broad knowledge in the rules and strategies of sports but does not have the same physical and athletic abilities as the actual players. Who would you want to have on the mound or at the plate in the ninth inning of a baseball game, the superstar athlete or the world-renowned commentator?

CHAPTER TWO

The Negative Black Subculture

Forty-eight percent of African Americans live in deteriorated inner-city neighborhoods with substandard housing and schools. They are isolated from conventional society and are faced with a constant assault on their self-image and sense of worth. The social forces operating in lower-class, inner-city areas produce high crime rates. What are these forces, and how do they produce crime?

These conditions have created the ultimate social disorganization and cultural deviance, which is the development of an independent lower-class negative subculture with a unique set of values, beliefs, and traditions that are distinct from conventional society. This subculture is plagued with self-destructive activity that helps shape behavior that influences daily activities. Its social norms also contribute to high rates of illegitimate children, domestic violence, crime, and drug use. Its members' way of life is centered on disregard for others, excessive consumption of drugs and alcohol, and senseless and destructive behavior within their own communities marked with apathy, cynicism, helplessness, distrust, and anger. This subcultural lifestyle can be passed from one generation to the next, becoming part of a permanent underclass. This is referred to as a cultural continuation. These areas are racially segregated, which continues to divide the population into two separate and unequal cultures in society. Members are chronically un-employed and stand by their motto, "The working man is a sucker." Because public assistance, government subsidies, and other entitlements are their primary means of income, the job market or an economic slowdown means little to nothing to their already existing condition. The fact that a small percentage of African Americans live in these conditions can help explain the distinct racial patterns in the national crime rate throughout various African American communities.

Within this negative subculture are separate groups with other sets of negative norms and principles. The members of these *criminal subcultures* operate in direct opposition to the conventional African American culture—for example, looters during protests and demonstrations. There is also a subculture of violence whose members engage in senseless and destructive antisocial acts, such as the knockout game. Their way of life is based on acts of pleasure and self-gratification, living for today by committing crimes, consuming drugs and alcohol, and engaging in reckless sexual activity. They resist efforts by family members, the clergy, and those in authority to control their behavior and instead embrace other negative groups. They measure their success based on elements of the value system they've created, such as producing the most children out of wedlock with multiple women, being the number-one producer and supplier of controlled substances and being feared for committing serious acts of violence against others within and outside of their own community. The negative subculture constantly behaves rebelliously against the police, teachers, social workers, merchants, potential employers, and all who follow conventional societal norms.

The lower-class or underprivileged in these disorganized neighborhoods throughout the country should not be stereotyped, categorized, or confused with the negative subculture groups. Those in the lower-class trying to survive in these communities' experience anger and frustration because they lack the ability to achieve legitimate social and financial success. They become frustrated because opportunities are not easily available while they are surrounded by many distractions. With no accessible means of obtaining success, they may fall to desperate measures, using methods of negative sub-cultures for obtaining financial status. When members of the lower-class group are unable to fulfill their ambitions and dreams because of their status, they tend to become influenced by the negativity in their surroundings.

Members of the lower-class and members of the subculture criminal class are separate groups that do not share a common value system that emphasizes cohesion within their community. The lower-class group strives to attain goals using conventional methods that result in gaining status when opportunities are lacking in their communities and difficult to obtain. The members of the negative subculture reject conventional goals and choose to live negatively while taking delight in the discomfort of others, making an obvious attempt to flout others in their community trying to achieve a legitimate status. These neighborhoods are unable to realize the common values of the lower-class residents due to the deviant social structure created by the negative subculture. The lower-class group feels significant levels of fear, intimidation, social dissatisfaction, and alienation from the rest of society. All or some of the negative subculture's behaviors and lifestyles may exist in various communities. These various social groups are segments of the population whose members may have similar attitudes, values, norms, and characteristics. These groups can be identified within the rich, upper, middle, or lower-classes, with a broad range of socio-economic variations in each group. These individuals can be transient due to a sudden change in their economic status, such as becoming an entertainer, professional athlete, established drug dealer, or lottery winner. You know that old saying: "You can take the boy out of the hood, but you can't take the hood out of the boy."

It would seem reasonable to conclude that individual acts of violence are motivated by some mental or psychological abnormality that one is suffering or has suffered and endured over a long period of time. When the abnormality becomes an essential part of the norm, people become prone to violence due to the negative atmosphere. Mental health experts talk about the importance of mental health treatment for war veterans and others like the Sandy Hook school shooting survivors: parents, school staff, and even emergency response workers who have been affected by this horrific act. Another tragic incident involved two school buses that collided in Knoxville, Tennessee. Two children and one adult were killed because of this accident. Schools were closed, and counselors were brought into offer psychological counseling.

Let's try to somewhat simplify black-on-black crime. Black-on-black crime refers to crime committed by African

Americans when the victim is another member of the same ethnicity. It specifically refers to violent crime, such as murder and assault, and includes gun-related crimes, such as armed robbery and malicious wounding. Why are the people in these communities so violent? From the time blacks were brought to this country and filtered into slavery, they endured the most horrific treatment. Following the end of slavery, during the Reconstruction process, newly freed slaves were in limbo. In a state of desperation, many blacks were forced to return to deplorable conditions, having no way to survive. With no education, no property, and no possessions other than the shirts on their backs, they had to fend for themselves. Segregated neighborhoods throughout various regions of the country became the genesis of black communities. Unlike a conventional community, these sections of unstructured ghettos were created to isolate a certain group of people from mainstream America. I don't think we need to go back down memory lane to murder, mob lynching, cross burnings, destruction of property, menacing, and coercion—the list goes on. Do we even need to mention the Jim Crow laws of the past? We need to emphasize environmental conditions; the relationship between crime, the physical, and the mental traits that were neglected over an extended period. The past has dictated the current conditions in which many of these people act on their own free will and choose between conventional or criminal behavior. For many individuals of the negative subculture, criminal activity is more attractive because it requires less effort for greater gain. Looting and burning businesses in these communities have no planned strategy and are opportunistic. These acts of destruction are confirmation to all that a negative climate exists within the community. This is the residual effects of slavery and those who were abused during that time and never treated for their Post-Traumatic Stress Disorder (PTSD).

America needs to research and study why the negative black subculture commits crime and how to end its destructive patterns. One of the major goals of criminologists, sociologists, and psychologists is to develop an understanding of the nature and cause of this negative subculture. Without knowing why and how it exists, it is extremely difficult to create effective solutions for antisocial behavior and crime. We will not be sure if efforts are being aimed at the proper groups or if they are effective. For example, if a crime preventive measure is providing jobs for the unemployed in a community, providing jobs for those individuals will only be effective in reducing crime if it is linked to unemployment. If an individual has adapted to a culture where becoming gainfully employed is purposely rejected, a job will not be the solution for this individual. The levels of disorder are complexed and varies between individuals and groups, some having multiple behavioral abnormalities. For example, an individual in a community who is a repeated criminal offender and rejects the conventional norms and customs of society such as employment, education, and religion, compounded with drug abuse and alcohol addiction, can and will create havoc in any community. In addition to understanding the nature and cause of this behavior, it is very important for the government to study and understand the role of these subjects. Such knowledge is essential for developing strategies to eliminate or reduce the probability of this type of behavior while providing information that these communities can use to decrease their likelihood of becoming a negative productive individual. We need to ask several fundamental questions. How do people develop into a negative, abnormal behavioral culture? What are the social, psychological, physical, and economical factors relating to this type of behavior? Is it a matter of free will, or do these people conform to the external forces of the environment? Do these individuals become victims of crimes because they are in the wrong place at the wrong time, or do their lifestyles of crime control their destiny?

The true burden to the lower-class is the development of the criminal culture. The individuals from the negative criminal culture, people who commit crimes and serious theft offenses, live within the lower-class communities. Most of all serious crimes occur in the inner-city areas within lower-class communities. The social forces operating in the lower-class, inner-city areas produce high crime rates. The negative black *criminal subculture* is the force that produces crime, not the lower-class group. The negative black *criminal subculture* is the product of the community that is both deteriorating physically and maintaining conflicting values and social systems. Lower-class neighborhoods are crime prone areas because their social institutions cannot function properly due to the negative black *criminal subculture's* social attributes. The negative black subculture is so prone to crime that the lower-class's social institutions cannot function properly. Due to the negative surrounding conditions, society is unable to realize the common values of the residents in these areas. An individual from the lower-class should not be mistaken for or categorized as someone from the negative *criminal subculture*. They come from two separate classifications living within the same geographical area. The lower-class values education and employment, works hard, and is active with family and religious communities. On the contrary, the negative black subculture applauds goals that are realistically obtainable in a negative, disorganized society.

Communities housing individuals from the negative black subculture experience high drug and alcohol use, have large numbers of single-parent households and large numbers of children born out of wedlock, and scoff at employment and education. They have an admiration for those who engage in criminal activities while scorning the police and others in authoritative positions. These negative black subculture values are incorporated into an active code of behavior such as not "snitching" or cooperating with law enforcement and joining a gang. The burden of the negative black subculture in the lower-class community has produced a negative set of values that conflicts with conventional rules and laws. Obedience to these negative values creates a community atmosphere of cohesion and support toward disobeying the rules of conventional society. The result is a high rate of crime and violence within the community. The problem with decaying inter-cultural neighborhoods is so overwhelming that numerous efforts are ineffective due to the social problems ingrained in these areas. People are committing crimes because of the experiences they have due to the conditions of the environment as well as how they are being socialized by the government, the media, and the rest of society. Those living in deficient communities are more strongly influenced toward criminal behavior by a poor family structure and support system, destructive peer groups, a lack of education, and aggressive and harsh treatment by law enforcement and the criminal justice system.

In the *criminal subculture*, many children are raised without the active participation of a father or positive male role model. Many young males fail to learn appropriate adult male behaviors due to the absence of the positive male figure. The *criminal subculture* male teaches negative male standards that are admired in this culture. These negative qualities and abilities include fighting skills, abusive treatment to women, toughness, street smarts, criminal activity, and so on.

Examine the classification chart below that describes or identifies the various groups of people within the negative criminal culture:

A = Extremely Dangerous / Menace to Society: those who identify themselves with their way of life as a normal negative standard way of surviving within their culture, such as a gang member.

B = The Hidden Nuisance: those who operate in the shadows, knowing right from wrong. They share common views within their negative culture but conceal themselves from sight to prevent themselves from being seen or identified as the same.

C = The Unproductive: those who have no aspirations to work or contribute to society in a positive manner. They purposely avoid productivity while seeking entitlements and other freebies.

Once again, crime rates, particularly black-on-black crime, can be linked to the lower-class social structure most common in the inner cities. Individuals who have limited access to desired goods through conventional means will often resort to illegal behavior and activities. When people believe that their unconventional negative cultural values are normal, a significantly higher crime rate will consume that community. Those living in conflicting cultural environments will attract disproportionate amounts of violence and crime. The higher crime rates in these lower-class communities are the results of those engaging in criminally acceptable behavior, which creates a positive self-image, as they view themselves as accomplished or successful in their abnormal culture. If statistical data show that blacks and other minorities make up a disproportionate amount of criminal activity, it is important to consider several other factors than race alone. When examining the lower-class and negative criminal coexisting cultures, evidence seems to suggest that serious crimes are more prevalent among the *criminal subculture*, while less serious crimes are even throughout the lower-class social structure. Education, unemployment, substance abuse, poverty, and other resource deprivations are all associated with crime and the abnormal culture.

Crime rates are higher in lower-class communities, but poverty alone cannot explain why particular groups or individuals become a chronic product of violence and other criminal activities. The *criminal subculture* has become a common and disturbing way of life in lower-class areas, particularly within the inner cities of the United States. The various sources of data about things such as public housing, public assistance, and drug treatment, along with criminal statistical data, tell us a lot about the nature, product, source, and patterns of crime.

CHAPTER THREE

Discretion or Discrimination

Blacks and other minorities must cope with both crime and the criminal justice system much more than whites, with devastating effects on their safety. Does American law enforcement intensify the problem by discriminating against minorities? Do blacks and minorities commit a disproportionate amount of crimes? Does the criminal justice system treat minorities differently from whites? If so, how can this be corrected? Time and time again, research has addressed the possibility of racial discrimination. Studies along with statistical data have offered evidence that racial bias in police stops, unwarranted searches, and arrest rates exists. The following information and data represent law enforcement only. There are numerous racial disparities when examining data, including different rates of prosecution, conviction, sentencing, incarceration, and parole. There are many reasons for these contradictions, which I will explain. The U.S. criminal justice system allows the police, prosecutors, and judges a great deal of discretion in handling criminal cases. Once again, we're scrutinizing the police, which is the initial point of contact an individual has with the criminal justice system.

I recall early in my career meeting with a sergeant to give him a police report that I had just completed. The report was related to a larceny from a vehicle.

The victim discovered that an unknown individual had entered his vehicle during the night. This area was located downtown in a business district. While waiting on the sergeant, the traffic in the area was extremely light, as the businesses in the immediate area had not begun to open. This section of town was still recovering from the nightlife. Litter drifted down the streets slowly as a light wind blew debris from place to place. Sporadically, people were moving about to start their day. The sergeant finally arrived, meeting me in the empty parking lot of a closed lounge. As he was scanning the report to make sure that I had completed all the essential information, we briefly talked about what the scene may have looked like a few hours earlier. While we were exchanging information on how we visualized the area during those peak hours, a citizen happened to walk by, utilizing the sidewalk on the opposite side of the street. The sergeant glanced up away from the report for a moment and happened to observe the male subject walking past. He stared momentarily at the subject and said to me, "That's the shithead that probably stole the stuff from out of this car," referring to the report he was reading. He said, "I should stop him." Being the new, naïve officer shortly out of the academy, I asked him how he could do that. "Why," I said, "what did he do?" He looked at me as if I were some stupid rookie and said, "You've got a lot to learn about this job."

He then continued to explain that I have the authority to stop someone anytime I feel like it. He told me to know what I can and can't do, and how to justify it. As I sat there in my marked police cruiser getting street knowledge from a veteran cop about how to stop anyone at any given time, I began to realize that there were a few clever ways of operating and performing certain activities that are slightly dishonest and unfair but were to my advantage. As I sat there with a puzzled look on my face, the sergeant said, "Listen carefully to what I'm about to ask you." He glanced away momentarily, looking straight ahead as if trying to figure out how to explain that I had inherited some sort of magical power, like Superman. He began to speak but would not look me in my eyes. He told me to carefully visualize the example that he was about to describe to me. He began by telling me to picture myself conducting a surveillance of a known location that has been burglarized numerous times in the past. While observing the front of this location from a hidden spot, I observe a subject drive up to the front door and quickly exit a vehicle. The subject appears to be a black male wearing dark clothing, work boots, and a hat with a brim that is pulled down, covering a portion of his upper face. The subject sprints to the glass door with an unknown object in his hand and begins pulling on it. After a couple of unsuccessful attempts at the door, the subject quickly walks to the adjacent door, looking through the glass. The subject returns to the first set of doors after seeing no one present next door. The subject then walks to the side of the building, where he begins pulling on a side glass door. After a third tug to the door, it finally opens, and the subject goes inside. The sergeant said, "Okay, based on the information that I have just relayed to you, would you say that it was enough for you to stop that subject?" I said, "Yes." He replied, "Exactly!"

The sergeant then directed me to turn around and look across the street. As I was looking in the direction I was directed to, I had no idea what I was looking for. I asked the sergeant; he said, "Just wait for a minute and keep looking." At that moment, a United Postal Service (UPS) worker exited the side door of the location described, following the delivery of a package. It was at that moment when the sergeant said to me, "you can make anything look like anything." He explained that, "I have the authority to do whatever I want." Here I am a young, new rookie police officer trying to tell my veteran police sergeant how it's supposed to be. I tried telling him that was not what we learned in the academy. I told him that the commonwealth (district) attorney lectured us on lawful stops and probable cause. I then saw the rage in his eyes. Becoming angry with me, he stated, "You don't know what the fuck you're talking about—watch me!"

He sped away, driving approximately a hundred feet before jumping out of his police cruiser. He approached a black male who was walking toward the sergeant when he exited the police car. As I approached them, I made sure to stay close to see and understand what was happening. I could see the male subject taking his hands out of his pockets and holding them down but extended from his body. As I neared them, I could hear the sergeant asking the subject why he was in the area and if he had any identification. The male stated that he had his identification (ID) card, while the sergeant began searching him. The subject stated that he was passing through the area to go downtown in the shopping district to get a haircut at a place approx- imately two miles away. The subject gave the sergeant a driver's license and then asked, "What did I do?" The sergeant told the subject that an individual was robbed nearby and that he fit the description. The sergeant went on to tell the subject that if he didn't do anything wrong, he had nothing to worry about. The sergeant began running the subject's information through the criminal justice radio communications system (CJRCS). Through- out the whole ordeal, the male subject was looking at me as to say, "You know this shit is foul; and this is who you roll with."

During the awkward moment of silence, the radio dispatcher communicated back to the sergeant, stating that the subject's license was valid and that he had no pending warrants on file. The sergeant handed the subject back his license and said, "Thank you, have a nice day," while staring him down firmly. When the subject walked out of earshot, the sergeant said to me, "No warrants—no weapons! You can do whatever the fuck you want. Like I said, you got a lot to learn." He drove off.

Police discretion gives law enforcement personnel the ability to enforce the law selectively. Officers have a great deal of latitude to use their discretion in deciding whether to invoke their power of authority or not. Discretion includes the ability of personal decision making about whether to take formal action or not. Police officers use a high degree of personal discretion when enforcing the law. The police are neither regulated in their daily procedures by government scrutiny nor subject to administrative review regarding discretion. The exercise of discretion by police often deteriorates into discrimination, violence, and other abusive practices. For example, while in an area known for its tourism, I observed a group of *plain clothes officers* assigned to this detail randomly stop individuals and request to see their identification. During the stop, the officers would explain that the location was a highly targeted area for terrorism and they were taking all precautions. The officers would then transmit the subject's information via radio through the National Crime Information Center (NCIC), checking for warrants while compiling data on these individuals. While observing the officers' interactions with various subjects in this area, I noticed that the subjects were all minorities. White subjects were not stopped as they traveled through the area. If you were to examine the numerous radio transmissions made during that period by those officers, the information recorded would reveal that the people were being stopped in a discriminatory manner.

Police officers have broad powers, and yet they operate with internal oversight and no punitive repercussions. This combination of power and the lack of accountability makes discrimination, *excessive force*, coercion, menacing behavior, abusive language, unjustifiable *deadly force*, and civil rights violations a widespread problem. In fact, given the nature of American policing, there is no surprise regarding the violence and the abusive relationship between the police and minorities. Discrimination is an issue, not simply because it means that all police officers are racist, but because it raises the question of who controls the police and what fair legal recourse there is. Public fears of police discrimination are because *excessive force* and *deadly force* are out of control.

Statistical data and numerous studies have shown that African Americans, Latinos, and other minority groups are likely to encounter the police due to racial profiling. Not only do minorities get stopped more often than whites, but they are also treated unfavorably. According to the Bureau of Justice Statistics (BJS), 3.6 percent of whites are searched compared to 9.5 percent of blacks and 8.8 percent of Latinos. Minorities are more likely to be arrested and more often experience some sort of unwarranted or *excessive force* during their encounter.

Example: Stop-and-Frisk in NYC

An analysis by the New York Civil Liberties Union (NYCLU) revealed that innocent New Yorkers have been subjected to police stops and street inter-rogations more than four million times since 2002 and that black and Latino communities continue to be the overwhelming target of these tactics.

Nearly *nine out of ten stopped-and-frisked New Yorkers have been completely innocent*, according to the NYPD's own reports from 2010 to 2013.

In 2010, New Yorkers were stopped by the police 601,285 times.
518,849 were totally innocent (86 percent).
315,083 were black (54 percent).
189,326 were Latino (33 percent).

54,810 were white (9 percent).

295,902 were aged fourteen to twenty-four (49 percent).

In 2011, New Yorkers were stopped by the police 685,724 times.

605,328 were totally innocent (88 percent).

350,743 were black (53 percent).

223,740 were Latino (34 percent).

61,805 were white (9 percent).

341,581 were aged fourteen to twenty-four (51 percent).

In 2012, New Yorkers were stopped by the police 532,911 times.

473,644 were totally innocent (89 percent).

284,229 were black (55 percent).

165,140 were Latino (32 percent).

50,366 were white (10 percent).

In 2013, New Yorkers were stopped by the police 191,558 times.

169,252 were totally innocent (88 percent).

104,958 were black (56 percent).

55,191 were Latino (29 percent).

20,877 were white (11 percent).

According to the New York Daily News (2017), the City of New York has agreed to pay up to $75 million in a class-action lawsuit settlement involving the NYPD's reckless behavior. Officers were accused of stopping and arresting individuals regardless of whether a violation or criminal act was committed. Officers were allegedly arresting people and issuing summonses without probable cause to meet quotas. Approximately nine hundred thousand summonses were dismissed on the grounds of being factually inadequate ranging over an almost nine-year period.

It is evident that the government is not sensitive enough relating to issues that are considerably important to minorities, such as the misuse of police power, unfair application of the law, and discriminatory practices by the police and the judicial system. The unequal enforcement of the law violates the Constitution's doctrines of equal pro-tection. While charges of police abuse continue to be made against police departments across the country, the evidence suggests that actual incidents of physical and verbal abuse of citizens by police officers are more frequent and expected. If the problem continues to be ignored, incidents will continue, police departments will pay more in civil and punitive damages, and more lives will be lost.

Police discretion is one of the reasons behind what many people see as racial profiling. Police officers are not formally trained to use discretion, as it's often believed that minorities are more likely to come from poverty-stricken areas and to be connected to criminal activities, which factors into police aggres-siveness. While racial profiling is illegal, and the use of police discretion is not a clear cut, exact science with specific rules, it is extremely difficult to prove racial profiling in a court of law. Racial profiling is a huge problem, as law enforcement continues to target individuals based on race, ethnicity, sexual orientation, national origin, and religion. While citizens are continuously humiliated by unlawful detentions and searches without cause or evidence of criminal activity, law enforcement will continue to lose credibility and trust among the communities they serve. Law enforcement targeting a group of individuals based not on their behavior but rather on their personal characteristics is a common practice. Some all-too-common racial profiling stops include black and Latino males who drive expensive automobiles being stopped by police or security while entering or exiting luxury condominiums or middle and upper-class neighborhoods, and they are often followed by security or loss-prevention personnel while in commercial establishments.

Let us closely examine when and how many minorities are constantly stopped by law enforcement. The initial contact should involve an act or incident that makes a person the subject of interest to law enforcement. In most instances, the initial contact is the result of a police action that should not be based solely on race or location. An arrest is considered legal when certain elements are present.

> **Probable cause** exists when facts and circumstances within a police officer's knowledge would lead a reasonable person to believe that the suspect has committed, is committing, or is about to commit a crime. Probable cause must come from specific facts and circumstances only. The actions of police officers

arresting subjects merely based on hunches and suspicions do not fulfill legal requirements. Another element of an arrest is when the officer deprives the individual of his or her freedom and the individual believe that he or she is now in police custody and is not free to leave.

Reasonable suspicion must be based on specific and articulable facts and circumstances, taken together with rational inferences from those facts and associated with the specific individual. Reasonable suspicion is a legal standard that is less than probable cause but more than just a mere hunch or suspicion. Police officers stopping individuals should be able to point to specific facts or circumstances connecting persons thought to be involved in criminal activity. The level of suspicion is less than probable cause, but more than a feeling or guess based on intuition or race than known facts.

Stop-and-frisk is when police officers who are suspicious of an individual run their hands lightly over the suspect's outer garments to determine if the person is carrying a concealed weapon. Police officers who confront and engage citizens on the streets do not always do this during or after an arrest. Officers frequently stop persons whom they say appear to be acting in a suspicious manner. Many police stops are related to citizen complaint calls about unknown subjects in certain areas. The police are not required to have sufficient evidence for an arrest to stop a person for brief questioning. The police have the legal authority to stop a person and ask questions while conducting a search in a limited way, as in the case of *Terry v. Ohio* (1968). This type of search is conducted as frisking for concealed weapons. These limited stop, question, and frisk encounters enable police officers to investigate suspicious persons and situations without having to meet any probable cause standard for arrest. Because of the extensive police authority and the lack of scrutiny and accountability, many innocent individuals are stopped fraudulently without cause.

Police violence, including *deadly force* and abuse of power, occurs in many localities across America with no sound method to control or eliminate the problem. Although most police officers are not violent and dangerous to the public, the many that are dangerous continue to bring discredit to policing. The lack of police accountability has created an enormous tension between the police and the communities they serve. Police abuse can include a few different things, such as un-warranted *deadly force*, unnecessary *use of force*, curse and abuse, and unreasonable searches, to name a few. In a newly surfaced YouTube video titled, "Racist female cop acts like gangster," you hear a white female officer tell a black male motorist that she can stop and pull him out of his vehicle and search him. The officer continues to state that she knows that she's unable to use whatever she finds because of the search because she understands her conduct is illegal.

I have known many police officers to randomly stop individuals and conduct illegal searches because they can do it without any consequences for their inappropriate behavior. There must be a legal recourse for the unlawful stops alone so that citizen complaints are heard, and officers' actions will be considered. An immediate plan to search for appropriate legal vehicles to bring law enforcement officers' actions before the state and federal court system is paramount. The concept of search and seizure along with cruel and unusual punishment can be found in the U.S. Constitution protecting all. When the conduct of law enforcement degrades the dignity of human beings, particularly minorities, and is fundamentally unfair, imminent action is needed. I have consulted many attorneys about civil suits that citizens may want to pursue regarding random unlawful stops by officers. I've explained the various stops in which subjects are searched, checked for warrants, told to leave areas, and threatened with arrests if they fail to do so. I have been told time and time again that the individual stopped has suffered no loss because of the officer's acts. Basically, no arrest and no legal recourse underscores the importance of protecting citizens from government. The best way to do this is to establish punitive guidelines in addition to the Bill of Rights and the U.S. Constitution to control the powers of law enforcement. Individuals must have certain rights whenever they are approached by police, and they must be able to act against officers who act outside of the law.

I have also known police officers to pull over subjects without probable cause when they have committed no offense. I've heard officers discuss how they stop individuals to locate wanted subjects and contraband. I've had one officer describe how he searched a person's vehicle without permission and sent him on his way after failing to find any illegal items. This officer went on to say how he would write traffic tickets to those motorists who complained about the stops. The officer said this was his way of covering himself in the event of any formal complaints relating to the stops.

I recall standing downtown in the business district with a jacket over my police uniform. I arrived to work early and had not begun my shift. It was a beautiful sunny day, and lots of people were out shopping. The traffic was moderate, and the sidewalks were filled with merchant seekers. As I stood in front of a shoe store watching people walk up and down the strip, I noticed a young black teenage male accompanied with a black female approximately the same age. The teenage couple were about thirty to fifty feet away, standing close to the sidewalk talking loudly while using all sorts of profane language. While standing there for approximately fifteen to twenty minutes, I heard the back and forth conversation between the male and female. The whole dialogue of the conversation consisted of drugs, fighting, money, and who is sleeping with whom. He then looked at me and said, "What the fuck are you looking at?" I thought to myself, this is exactly what a negative *criminal subculture* subject looks and acts like. "Perhaps a person who dropped out of school and has no education, someone with a criminal record, someone who has been arrested multiple times, someone who frequents jail, someone who is a drug user or abuser, someone who wears his pants extremely low to the point where his drawers are showing, someone without a job, someone who receives public assistance, lives in public housing, and wreaks havoc on the complex while using foul language, someone who drinks and urinates in public, someone who was created out of wedlock, someone who grew up without a father, someone who disrespects others including the elderly and anyone else." I shook my head and walked away when he replied, "Fuck you!"

The point I'm trying to make telling this story is simply how: (a) I did not aggressively approach this individual to the point of escalating a situation that could turn violent; (b) I began processing the character, conduct, and threat level of the subject; and (c) I de-escalated the interaction to the point that no physical acts of danger were warranted. I want to emphasize the technique of processing the character and demeanor of individuals who police officers encounter.

Ongoing national footage and violent videos of widely publicized incidents of police brutality continue to plague departments and agencies around the country. Numerous deadly shooting cases continue to focus attention on alleged increases in police brutality. Curbing police brutality will be very difficult if it is not acknowledged as a systemic problem deeply rooted in the core values of American policing. A more rigorous psychological vetting process is paramount to eliminate potentially violent police candidates. The need for a sophisticated monitoring system of police behavior in situations involving *use of force* and violence will help identify potentially violent officers so they can be removed from the public. A more pragmatic approach to curbing police brutality and excessive *deadly force* is to enforce detailed rules of engagement that limit officers' *use of force*; such rules are outlined in the policies of many law enforcement agencies' standard of procedures manuals. Many of the police policies and training methods that are used by police agencies are designed to prevent excessive and *deadly force.* For example, let's look at the Tamir Rice shooting in Cleveland, where a Cleveland police officer shot and killed a twelve-year-old boy as he played with a toy pellet gun in a public park outside of a recreation center. The responding officers immediately drove into the *kill zone* of a potential armed subject. One officer exited his vehicle and fired a shot, killing the subject within seconds of exiting the patrol unit. An Ohio grand jury decided not to indict the officers.

We understand that police departments have developed training methods that consider how officers function under adverse conditions and in certain situations. But, whatever happened to *tactical positioning* and containment, interaction of human perception along with threat assessment, communication and verbal command, and patrol response de-escalation and defusing techniques? I am very confident that the way the officers responded will not be found in any training manual in the United States. Any time an officer violates policy and procedures outlined by his department, he should be held accountable for his actions. Liabilities should not make officers immune to criminal and civil consequences.

Attached at the end of this chapter is a copy of the Cleveland Police Department's general order regarding their *use of force* policy. Take a close look at section III, force level A and B, one through five. It states how officers should first attempt to use verbal commands and warnings to gain compliance. If this tactic is not successful, call for additional units to create a show of force. Members should consider alternative tactics than the *use of force*, such as *tactical positioning*, concealment, cover, continuous voice commands, and other verbal attempts of de-escalation. And finally, it explains the importance of having good judgment and acting carefully to allow time for people to gain control and cease struggling or resisting when their actions do not immediately threaten the safety of others.

Recommendation:

When a law enforcement officer engages in conduct that violates departmental policies and procedures outlined by the agency of employment, the officer should be held liable for negligence or incompetence, which can be defined as malpractice. Due to the reckless behavior of members in law enforcement, many localities have paid and will continue to pay out resulting from liability lawsuits. All individuals in law enforcement should be required to obtain liability insurance and maintain such insurance for the duration of employment as a condition to practice law enforcement. Each law enforcement officer will be required to purchase his or her own active policy. The premiums will vary based upon an individual's work conduct and history. No longer will officers practice law enforcement with a blank liability open checkbook. The more the violations, the higher the premiums. The higher the premiums, the lower one's salary. If an officer is reckless in his behavior, his premiums will eventually be so high that he will force himself to correct his behavior. An officer may even be forced to forfeit the terms of his employment when he fails to obtain liability insurance because he is a risk and companies refuse to insure him.

Police officers routinely stop citizens without cause to check for warrants, a suspended license, weapons, drugs, and other illegal contraband. These unlawful searches and seizures conducted by law enforcement officers are acts that have exceeded the scope of police authority. Unreasonable searches and seizures are those for which law enforcement officers did not have sufficient information to justify their actions. I've asked several attorney acquaintances about officers stopping citizens without cause and letting them go. The answer that I've received from each attorney was the same. They all have unanimously stated that the individual who has been stopped can file a complaint with the officer's department but has no legal recourse because there was no loss due to the stop. The attorneys defined a loss as an illegal arrest and a search associated with a seizure. In other words, you can be stopped, searched, and sent on your way with no recourse other than to file a police complaint, which will be investigated by the police department and almost always declared unfounded.

The provisions in the Fourth Amendment clearly state that no warrant shall be issued without probable cause. A warrant may be written only when such request is supported by facts that convince the court or a magistrate that a crime has been or is being committed. It is important to understand the difference between a written warrant by a judge and warrantless searches. The warrantless search is a lawful search incident to arrest. When stopped by police, always ask, "Am I under arrest, or am I free to leave?" An arrest occurs if a person believes he or she cannot leave, and the officer conveys this to the individual. In other words, a person is not seized under the Fourth Amendment until he or she either has been subjected to some type of physical force or has submitted to the assertion of government control. The officer is always given the benefit of the doubt in court relating to testimony. Therefore, give yourself the benefit of the doubt and ask the officer if you are free to leave or under arrest with your cellular phone in record mode.

CHAPTER FOUR

Protect Us, or Police Them

Policing in America is a vehicle used to control blacks, Latinos, immigrants, members of the LGBT community, the poor, interracial couples, and others alike. A community's racial makeup influences police behavior. The degree of authority an officer exercises is defined by the working environment he is assigned. Police in predominantly white communities have been found to make the highest use of discretion and punitive behavior toward minorities compared to whites. In fact, police in predominantly white neighborhoods and commercial areas were significantly more aggressive and punitive to black offenders than whites. Police commonly use formal arrest procedures more often in lower-class neighborhoods than in middle and upper-class neighborhoods. Police are more likely to take formal action in poor areas. It is also clear that a community's racial or ethnic makeup affects an officer's arrest decision making. An environmental factor affecting the police officer's performance is his or her perception of the people within that community. For example, officers will make statements such as, "They're on welfare and use up our tax dollars; they are criminals and don't deserve any [civil or constitutional] rights." Middle-class and working-class minority Americans frequently have negative interactions with the police due to law enforcement's inability to distinguish minorities from criminals. Law enforcement officer's stereotypical behavior instinctively supersedes their demeanor and behavioral processing skills. An individual's behavior and appearance are only a couple of the many characteristics the police should rely on during this critical assessment. Officers who fail to assess these factors methodically cause an automatic breakdown in communication with the potential of creating a volatile confrontation.

The practices and customs of American policing have an influence on the officer's behavior. Many policies designed to structure police behavior are in standard of operations procedure manuals assigned to all uniformed personnel. Police *use of force* is a serious problem; statutory policies that restrict inappropriate use of violence by police are needed as a control measure to deter what would be otherwise considered unlawful acts or hate crimes. Police officers are taught the proper methods in response to escalating levels of threats or force when dealing with individuals. The resistance ranges from compliant and cooperative to assaultive with threats of serious bodily harm to potential death. The appropriate force should be in conjunction with the threat level. The force ranges from verbal commands, contact control, compliance techniques, defensive tactics, and *deadly force*. Officers are taught in the academy through lecture, hands-on demonstration, and actual scenarios assessing suspects' behavior and applying the appropriate amount of force. An overwhelming number of citizens believe that the police discriminate against minorities. They use *excessive force* when handling suspects and display disrespect to innocent bystanders while engaging others.

While charges of police brutality are suddenly emerging from jurisdictions throughout the country due to technology, the evidence suggests that these actual incidents of physical and verbal abuse of citizens by police officers are far more frequent. With the aid of cellular telephone technology and the media attention given to numerous incidents, not only does race based police brutality occur more frequently against black and Latino citizens, but police officers have increased their violent interactions with citizens of all races, including whites. The force used by police against citizens and suspects detained is mostly punching, kicking, smacking, and shoving. The use of technology is having a significant impact on American policing and has only exacerbated the current conditions. Ask yourself two questions: What are some of the areas that technology will have an impact in policing? Why do the police detest being recorded in the act of performing their lawful duties? One would assume that such a recording would corroborate their account of events, which would strengthen their argument. Or do we conclude that their actions contradict their verbal or written testimony? All too often, minorities have made complaints about police brutality or some form of police misconduct to no avail due to the lack of evidence. Those who have made official complaints have often heard the outcome being "unfounded" or "unsubstantiated." If you believe the separate agencies and divisions within the criminal justice system operate independently, you are truly naïve. A significant number of video recordings have produced evidence indicating that racial bias does influence the decision to *stop-and-frisk* or initiate contact with subjects with few to no legal factors present. Racial influences on police stops are quite often subtle and hard to prove without technological support.

The internal affairs division (IAD) is charged with policing the police. It processes citizen complaints of excessive and unnecessary *use of force*, corruption, and other situations of actual criminal activity involving its own members. The IAD often assists police management personnel regarding disciplinary action brought against officers. Internal affairs are a controversial unit that is controlled by the command staff of the chief of police. Due to the lack of independence within, it is feared that influences from senior police officials often dictate the outcome of investigations.

Police are assigned to maintain order, enforce criminal law, answer radio calls for service, and handle traffic related matters, just to name a few. A police officer's duty requires discretion in several matters dealing with a variety of situations. The officer must determine if police action is necessary, whether a crime has been committed, and if there are victims, suspects, or witnesses, or refer someone to another agency for other services. Police officers normally use this methodical behavioral approach when dealing with white individuals, working according to a systematic and established form of procedure. Police officers assigned to low-income minority communities use the *aggressive behavioral approach* which tends to be irritable, impulsive, coercive, and condescending. This verbally abusive behavior combined with acts of aggression creates an atmosphere of tension that often leads to violent altercations.

Police behavior is learned through interactions with others. This type of learned aggression that is rewarded or not corrected becomes habitual. Officers act aggressively because, as rookies, they model their behavior after the assertive behaviors of senior officers and these patterns are reinforced by peers in the field. Officers who have learned this behavior and have seen it rewarded are more likely to react violently under normal circumstances. The officer's behavior during an initial interaction with a subject, whether it's a victim, a suspect, or just an ordinary citizen, will depend heavily on the subject's race. It is difficult to categorize every situational factor influencing behavior, but the two that stand out as having major significance are economic status and community.

The behavior of aggressive police officers is almost always reactionary against those whom they anticipate being noncompliant. These types of officers perceive others to be more aggressive than they are, creating an immediate maximum threat level. When they attack the targeted subject, they often say the individual was the aggressor and that they were effecting an arrest. These officers often lack behavioral/danger processing skills and cultural diversity, which often leads to misreading the situation (e.g., the Eric Garner case). Correcting police brutality will be difficult because it is rooted in the core values of policing and in American society. From slavery to the civil rights era, Americans have incorporated and applauded the *use of force*, coercion, and violence with justice. Police abuse of minorities in communities and in custody is not uncommon but is an all-too-familiar legal situation in American society. The current commonplace oppressive handling of minorities reflects these violent roots of the past. The way the police approach citizens makes a difference. The proactive aggressive stops used by police may help reduce crime in certain underprivileged minority communities but often fail to meet the legal requirements relating to the Fourth Amendment.

When an officer's actions are respectfully questioned, police violence will be ignited because officers view this as a challenge that defies their power and authority. If an individual is stopped by the police, he has no recourse other than to submit to their every demand, even if he knows his rights are being violated. Failing to comply, even without using any physical force at any time, will constitute a resisting arrest charge, subjecting you to excessive or even possibly *deadly force*. The *excessive force* used by police during the arrest process is a means of deterrence for future encounters and sends a message to others who may have an interaction as well. The objective is to inflict enough pain and fear in an individual to offset resistance at any time. These tactics are normally used in public view in front of other potential subjects, showing them that subjects who resist will not gain from their actions but only be punished. There is clearly a distinction between physically resisting with force and passively resisting by being uncooperative.

The system and process of criminal justice in the United States depend on effective, efficient, and impartial policing. This is extremely important when it comes to engaging citizens from all walks of life, whether preventing and detecting crime or apprehending and arresting individuals. Police officers must be fully competent to investigate crimes but must also be aware of laws, rules, and procedures associated with de-taining, arresting, apprehending, and investigating criminal activity in an unbiased manner. Police officers must be familiar with the facts involved while using the *methodical behavioral approach* which detects, screens, and processes information relating to potential offenders. A police officer's duties are controlled by legal boundaries governed by the U.S. Constitution and criminal procedure law. The police set the criminal justice system in motion with the authority to investigate, detain, arrest, and carry out a host of other lawful tasks. This authority should be vested with the strictest compliance in the law.

Police officers are required to make vital decisions on numerous matters dealing with a variety of situations that are detrimental to life with little room for error. The officer must not assume but determine whether it is lawful to stop and detain or appropriate to make an arrest. The arrest powers of the police involve taking individuals into custody in accordance with law. They have the authority to detain individuals to answer for a violation of the law. For an arrest to be lawful, there are a few legal requirements that must be fulfilled. A police officer must provide sufficient evidence, known as probable cause that a crime is being committed or has been committed and the suspect is the person who committed it. It is at this point that the officer detains the individual and deprives that person of his or her freedom, and the subject then believes that he or she is not free to leave and is now in the custody of the police. Unfortunately, a great number of blacks and other minorities are stopped by law enforcement every day for absolutely no legal reason.

According to an NYPD report on *stop-and-frisk*, approximately 88 percent of the stops from 2010 to 2013 were of innocent citizens; 87 percent of those individuals stopped were blacks and Latinos. These illegal encounters do not meet the legal requirements to arrest individuals. Do people have to stop for police when they have done nothing illegal? Are people obstructing the police or resisting arrest by not stopping? Are the police required to inform you why you are being stopped?

According to those same NYPD statistics, 187,858 whites were stopped during that same period. Do these stops violate the constitutional rights of individuals? Are there any consequences or repercussions resulting from these unlawful stops? What, if any, are the punitive damages due to individuals whose rights are violated? What measures are in place to make sure these acts do not continue? Will the police continue to police the police and declare these actual incidents unsubstantiated or unfounded? Or do the men and women of this almost great country stand up and fight for justice and freedom? Will the use of video recordings and other means of technology aid and assist the citizens of the United States when they are victims of police abuse of authority by means of unconstitutional stops and excessive and *deadly force*? Will prosecutors and district attorneys continue exercising malfeasance and nonfeasance using loopholes to manipulate grand juries and trials to get the outcomes they desire? Why do police advocates divert attention from police brutality by mentioning black-on-black crime?

Let's talk about both systemic and problematic conditions, which are entirely different. Police brutality involves behavior and actions such as abusive language, coercion, threats of violence, unnecessary *use of force*, *excessive force*, *deadly force*, stopping and searching individuals without cause to harass them, and so on. Police brutality exists all over the United States and can be in the form of a physical attack causing injury or death or a psychological attack involving mental abuse through intimidation. Various forms of police mis-conduct can include false arrest, racial profiling, and taking false statements and confessions using intimidation. While complaints of police brutality continue to be made in many police departments across the country, the evidence may suggest that these numerous instances of physical abuse of citizens by police officers have a racial pattern in comparison to a training issue.

Recommendation:

There is a need to create a significant source of criminal justice data relating to police behavior involving a *use of force* analysis of law enforcement activities. These records should be acquired covering a variety of fields and could be used for several purposes. These files can be analyzed to determine what types of complaints of abuse are occurring across the country. They can be examined and evaluated to determine the characteristic behavior of law enforcement officers who develop patterns of abuse and misconduct. The information will be an important source of behavioral data that is compiled and analyzed by the DOJ.

What will this data tell us about police departments across the country? Finding trends and patterns in police brutality will help us understand the nature of the source and plan control mechanisms. For example, if police statistical data show that police brutality is constantly coming from white officers against minorities in certain geographical areas, then the abuse may be a result of possible racial extremists who have infiltrated the police applicant process. If, in contrast, the police abuse is spread evenly across the country and the various ethnic makeup of officers, then there may be strong evidence that the abuse is linked to training.

We have entered a new (or should I say, "modern day"?) civil rights movement that believes strongly in political and social change. Its members take part in public protests and demonstrations against police brutality, demanding criminal justice reform. The Black Lives Matter organization is a group that campaigns against police brutality of African Americans. This organization was created by a few black activists and has attained national awareness with protests across the country following high profile shooting deaths of unarmed African Americans by police. This organization is decentralized, with no formal governing authority or structure. Due to the lack of police account-ability, the Black Lives Matter organization continues to grow in numbers while increasing in ethnic diversity. The movement highlights the disproportionate killings and violent attacks against African Americans by white officers.

The creation of a new group of activists called Police Brutality Matters is currently underway; it is being structured to assist the campaign against police brutality. This organization will help bring awareness to how policing is conducted within minority communities. This group will help explain the difference between aggressive policing, appropriate police practices, and justifiable shootings in the past and present. A major goal of this organization is to simply define police brutality versus crime and violence in low-income black communities. For example, police brutality occurs when a law enforce-ment officer uses excessive or unnecessary force against someone. This is beyond the force that is reasonable under the circumstances. Acts of police brutality are a violation of civil rights and criminal law. Force used by a police officer should be the minimum amount needed to effect an arrest or to achieve a legitimate purpose, such as restraining an emotionally disturbed person. The use of *excessive force* is a violation of certain amendments of the U.S. Constitution, such as the Fifth Amendment's due process of law and the Eighth Amendment's prohibition of cruel and unusual punishment.

Now, let's address the subject of so called black-on-black crime. There is no one single scientific explanation to describe the violent tendencies that plague almost all poor or low-income African American communities. I'll explain this in simple police *comp-stat* terms. The murder rate for black males is far higher than for any other group in the United States. A simple explanation is that crime is usually related to crime and poverty combined. People who live in poverty-stricken communities compounded with growing criminal social structures will be most likely to commit violent crimes. Not everyone living in these communities are violent or a criminal. Many low-income residents of these communities follow the conventional society standards of living while combatting the negative racial and criminal stereotyping from all outsiders, most notably the police. The fact that a small portion of African Americans live in these low-income public housing areas compared to the total population of African Americans can explain the distinct racial makeup of murder statistics geographically. To have a better understanding of which people are committing crimes against those closest to them, particularly in these deteriorated inner-city neighbor-hoods, use the pushpin method on maps of areas across the country to show these acts of violence. Many of these *criminal subculture* residents be-come victims of violence relating to their personal characteristics and lifestyle activities. Personal characteristics such as a criminal record, employment history, educational background, and substance abuse history are indicative of their lifestyle. Lifestyle activities are endless, ranging from drug distribution to ticket scalping on the street corner. The loss of life is tragic, no matter who the victim was or where the violent act occurred, but there are indicators that the likelihood of a crime occurring is often dependent on the victim's behavior.

The true questions are, how many of these troubled communities represent the total black population, and how can government fix this sociocultural dysfunction? How does one remove the negative elements from? low-income environments so that people who live in these communities can strive to achieve middle-class status? We need to first and foremost educate the country regarding stereotypes of African Americans and other ethnic groups. There is a troubling perception that blacks and Latinos, particularly males, commit violent crimes or are more likely to commit criminal acts abroad. Constant images in the media associate African Americans with criminal activities. It has been ingrained in the minds of so many that black-on-black crime is out of control when there are more white people victimized by whites than blacks victimized by blacks.

We need to conduct research to examine criminal data in the United States. Analyzing and understanding criminal statistics will aid scientists in developing strategic methods. For example, per capita, African Americans are much more likely to commit and be arrested for crimes of violence than other racial groups. They are also significantly more likely to be profiled, arrested, assaulted, convicted, and incarcerated than others who commit similar offenses. While African Americans make up less than one-fifth of the country's population (13 percent), they represent more than half of the country's prison population. One of the most important questions one should ask when conducting such research is, "Who are these groups of individuals, and where are they located?" We need to closely examine the areas in which they reside. It is also important to examine and collect data relating to police *use of force*. Such data will help track and measure the incidents and the number of use-of-force occurrences nationwide. Such data can determine an officer's department, agency, and locality, such as state, city, or town. It will also gather other information, including race, gender, age, and any other pertinent information that will be vital in minimizing brutality and holding those responsible accountable.

It is extremely difficult to accept the notion that training is the root of the problem concerning the use of *deadly force* by white male police officers against unarmed black males. The Department of Criminal Justice Services (DCJS) has developed training modules, known as the *use of force* continuum, that consider how all officers apply *use of force*. There is no separate training for officers of various ethnicities, genders, ages, heights, or weights. The *use of force* training is designed to teach officers the proper methods of escalating and deescalating force in response to the threats they may encounter in the field. *Use of force* training will present a variety of behaviors from subjects an officer may be confronted with, such as the various resistance ranges, from compliant and cooperative to assaultive and combative with the threat of serious bodily harm or death. Officers are taught through classroom lectures, demonstrations, and training videos of actual incidents, and they are tested during training scenarios. This training is vital in evaluating an officer's ability to assess a subject's behavior and apply only the appropriate and corresponding amount of force needed.

I cannot make this any clearer, the lack of cultural diversity, sensitivity, and acceptance is one of many reasons that the police have a poor relationship with minorities. Another problem to consider is the officers' perception of threat level when dealing with minorities. The level of force should correspond with a subject's behavior. The officer's *use of force* is determined by the amount of resistance he is receiving from an individual. For example, if a police officer confronts an individual who is compliant and cooperative (level 1), the officer's *use of force* should be verbal commands without physical force or abusive language. An individual who becomes passively resistant (level 2) will become subject to lawful contact control techniques, such as the grabbing of arms and legs to apply restraint devices such as handcuffs, leg irons, belly chains, and other such restraints. Someone who becomes resistant and violent (level 3) will be subject to defensive tactics and compliance techniques such as physical wrist and arm lock takedowns, applied force on pressure points, and strikes to various areas of the body known as stunning techniques, all to combat resistance. Also, departments across the country allow the use of aerosol oleoresin capsicum (OC) pepper spray, the baton or asp telescoping baton, and the electric control device known as the Taser, which falls under the same category as the takedown tactic and actual strikes. An officer's level of force should correspond to the level of a subject's resistance or fight that the individual is displaying. Officers should not rapidly progress through each level of force to reach the final level of *deadly force* when it does not correspond with a subject's actions. At no time should a progressive level of force be used by law enforcement as a means of retaliation, such as applying pepper spray for kicking the doors within a transport vehicle, using the Taser on someone who refuses to sign a summons, or striking someone over the head with a nightstick for hurling insults. Finally, subjects who are dangerous and violent and can cause serious bodily harm or death to an officer (level 4) can be subject to *deadly force*. *Deadly force* can be described as the authority and ability of a police officer to kill a suspect if the suspect presents a dangerous, life-threatening situation to the officer or the community. Police officers are not permitted to use *deadly force* against unarmed fleeing felons.

The government needs to identify, acknowledge, and create valid solutions for the causes of crime in low-income communities. Trying to pour money into the bottomless pit is not a solution to crime and dysfunction in troubled communities. Failing to utilize the training that law enforcement officers are provided with will result in excessive or *deadly force*, which can be criminal in nature. Officers cannot use catch phrases such as, *"I am in fear of my life"* when they have created the *deadly force* situation. Police training is an on-going process throughout an officer's career. While training begins at the police academy and is conducted by larger departments, smaller departments train their officers at regional training centers. Among the topics covered are criminal, civil, and constitutional law, firearms training and qualifications, emergency vehicle operations training, defensive tactics, *use of force*, and restraint techniques.

Profiling is the systematic arrangement of entities in a field into categories or classes based on common characteristics such as ideology, race, behavior, dress, dialogue, and so on, which can and will affect an individual's judgment and behavior. Labeling in policing is the description of individuals based on race, location, appearance, age, or some other visual characteristics rather than criminal behavior. Let's examine another classification chart below that describes or identifies various groups of people with cultural differences.

A = The Super Extremist one who identifies with a belief or doctrine relating to superiority over all other races to an extent well beyond the ordinary.

B = The Hidden Racist: one who operates in the shadows, or "stealth mode." This person shares multiple views with the extremist but conceals them from sight to prevent from being the same. This person is aware of injustice but fails to acknowledge it or justifies the behavior of those who support it.

C = The Denouncer: one who openly or publicly condemns or censures racist behavior but secretly has a natural or prevailing disposition toward unacceptable behaviors.

Many police officers will aggressively approach individuals based on the location and conditions of an environment. For example, an officer will approach a black male in an upper-middle-class building occupied by mostly white residents to inquire why he is there. With this type of behavior, police officers are not homed in on criminal acts or behavior but are more often making assumptions. It is quite common for police officers to randomly stop minorities and ask them, "Where are you going?" I have assisted many officers during traffic stops, and all too often, individuals are questioned regarding their travels. If someone refuses to answer such a question, he or she is severely chastised and threatened with either an obstruction or a disorderly charge. Officers will be little people excessively to the point where they become enraged, leading to an arrest.

Arrest power of police officers involves taking subjects into custody in accordance with the law. Individuals are held accountable for violations of criminal law. All arrests are normally initiated with or without warrants but should always be based on probable cause. Most of arrests are made by law enforcement without a warrant. The decision to arrest an individual is made by the police. Many police officers will arrest someone for resisting arrest without an initial charge. These bogus charges are always dropped by the prosecutor's office because they fail to meet legal requirements for a conviction. One must ask, "What law was originally violated to warrant a resisting arrest charge?"

February 13, 2014 Protestors rally against police brutality at Washington Sq. Park.

December 13, 2014 People from all walks of life gather to demand change in policing policies.

Joseph J. Ested

December 13, 2014 Supporters of Black Lives Matter gather at Washington Sq. Park during protest.

August 5, 2017 Centered is Joseph Ested, with Samaira Rice (L) and Gwen Carr (R) during an event in Atlanta, GA.

December 13, 2014 Approximately 25,000 protesters marched from Washington Sq. Park to mid-town Manhattan.

December 13, 2014 Protesters held signs while demanding criminal justice reform as they marched.

November 25, 2014 Police stand by while protesters gather to demand change.

November 25, 2014 Protesters block the entrance to the Lincoln Tunnel in NYC.

CHAPTER FIVE

Racism within the Blue Walls

Police departments across the country have tried to recruit minority police officers. The purpose of this effort is to create an illusion of a more balanced force that truly represents the community it serves. A more integrated looking department is an attempt to gain the public's confidence and convince them that police departments are not bigoted and biased organizations through a change in outward appearance.

Minority officers continue to suffer a great deal of discrimination. With a smaller chance of promotion, they're often assigned solely to patrol in the worst of the worst neighborhoods. In many instances in the past, minority officers would call white officers to various locations at the request of white citizens. White officers often hold prejudiced attitudes and frequently refuse to ride with minorities in patrol cars. Many specialized units are pre-dominantly controlled by white male officers. A huge and persistent problem is the difficulty that black officers and other minorities have in attaining command positions. Despite the increasing number of blacks and Latinos in supervisory positions, the percentage of minorities in the senior ranks lags substantially when compared to the total representation on police forces across the country. Many minority police organizations have been created and have filed lawsuits over transfers, assign-ments to specialized units, and promotion practices. Because

of the lack of diversity, courts have ordered departments to promote minorities so that the racial makeup
of the department's supervisory staff reflects the number of
minorities in the department. The legal action brought by
these minority organizations has often created a change to
increase minority representation.

Many police departments do not have any form
of civil service testing when seeking candidates to fill
vacancies in the rank of detective or other specialized
areas in policing such as K-9, motorcycle, harbor,
mounted, and aviation. Higher education has not been
associated with a more productive police officer in the
field. I will bet that statistics would indicate that a college
education does not improve police performance or
productivity. Many college educated officers throughout
the country generate more complaints and have difficulty
using discretion compared to their peers without college
degrees. Those with a higher education produce fewer
quality arrests, more on the job injuries, more citizen
complaints, more *excessive force* complaints, and more
disciplinary action. The most effective training and education
an officer can obtain is through life experience. Officers who
have lived in certain ethnic communities, learning cultures
and customs through day to day interactions, understand and communicate with others more effectively.
Having individuals in policing with higher education
does not actually predict effective performance in the
field. These so called "educated officers" tend to be better
report writers and exhibit above average technical skills
in the use of computers and Microsoft software. They are
articulate, communicate well during lectures, and can

research information using various database. On the other hand, they lack the good judgment, problem solving, reasoning, and common sense learned on the streets. They often speak to others in a condescending manner and tend to ridicule those who lack education. One factor to consider relating to the educated officer in the field is the escalating police misconduct complaints and the civil liability payouts. For example, the number of civil rights cases brought against the NYPD has increased by 70 percent since 2006 and cost the city $185 million in 2011.

The experience of blacks and other minorities in policing is quite complex. Because of the behavior within the *police culture*, minority officers often deal with the expectation from citizens of their own race that they will get a break while continuously witnessing overt racism from their fellow officers. Minority officers adapt to these pressures in ways that range from denying that blacks and other minority citizens are being treated differently from whites to treating minorities more aggressively than white citizens to prove their loyalty to their white colleagues. They are constantly seeking acceptance from whites in policing while they are particularly sensitive to any scrutiny or disrespect given to them by other minorities. Those minority officers who are less willing to accept these discriminatory practices by the department tend to be harassed, subjected to fabricated complaints and frivolous charges of misconduct resulting in harsh disciplinary action, and denied transfers and opportunities for promotion. Blacks and other minorities in law enforcement learn abusive behavior by watching others be rewarded for compliance with police misconduct and be punished for speaking in opposition to it. These officers imitate and model the behaviors that are rewarded. Rewards include receiving off-duty or outside depart-mental work and special assignments, being selected to specialized units, receiving promotional opportunities, and getting special exemptions from disciplinary action they may face. A great number of minority officers who interact in lower-class minority neighborhoods are insensitive to those living in these communities because they have conformed to the *police culture*. Many minority officers who fail to abide by the *police culture* norms and do not model their behavior this way is subjected to a great deal of abuse by police administrators.

Discrimination at the supervisory and management levels undisputedly precludes blacks, Latinos, and other minorities from changing the negative and abusive culture within. Racism in policing continues to exist despite the current trends of police departments across the country who hire African Americans to the positions of Chief or Commissioner, while the department's hierarchy continues to be exclusively dominated by those other than minorities. Quite often, in an environment made hostile by their peers, minorities are forced to perform their jobs under enormous pressure while attempting to gain others' acceptance by conforming closely to the norms and behavior of the culture. Many minorities in law enforcement who lack self-esteem try to be more loyal and tougher than expected, becoming excessively violent in minority communities. In many departments across the country, white superiors and officers alike congregate secretly, using offensive language referring to blacks and other minorities, including fellow officers. Minority officers are not only passed over for promotions and elite assignments to other units but are abused extensively for speaking out against racial injustice within the force. The treatment endured by many officers extends beyond the line of duty. Minority officers are often stopped by police while off duty and are subjected to the same ridicule and objectionable behaviors that are inflicted on everyday minority citizens until they identify themselves as police officers. From high ranking officers to veteran officers and detectives, many were driving or walking but not doing anything illegal when they were illegally stopped and aggressively detained. Numerous officers and citizens have produced secret recordings of such behavior by officers to no avail. Police personnel who produce such evidence are labeled snitches or traitors, making them fearful and reluctant to combat such behavior.

I recall my brother telling me about an incident he heard from a black sergeant in the police department where we were employed. The sergeant was traveling in his personal vehicle late at night in plain clothes while off duty when he was stopped by a white male police officer for no apparent reason. The white officer approached the sergeant while holding him at gunpoint and shouting commands. The sergeant explained that while this confrontation was occurring, he had his police uniform hanging upright against the rear passenger side window located behind the driver's seat. He claimed to have made an inquiry regarding the stop to the officer's supervisor, which led to nothing. The sergeant, who was perhaps afraid to make a formal complaint, was promoted to the rank of lieutenant at a much later time.

The fear of not getting transferred to specialized units or being promoted is another tactic used to control minority employees who formally complain or rock the boat. Any such complaints to police managers regarding racism or sexual harassment in any fashion are frowned upon by administrators. Minority officers who complain in any form are subjected to abuse and harassment by police administrators. This type of police administrative deterrence tactic (PADT) is a form of retaliatory behavior used as a deterrent to be inflicted on individuals who complain. The object is to apply enough abuse to individuals who complain to offset the amount of satisfaction gained from the complaint itself. This alarms other potential complainers by showing them that a punished individual will not gain from his or her actions. The speed at which punishment is applied is rather swift. The quicker a punishment for making a complaint is inflicted, the better the likelihood of preventing future complaints. Police administrators believe if an individual who makes a complaint is punished immediately, he or she will most likely be deterred then and in the future. They want minority officers to believe that if they make any such complaint of injustice within the department, division, or unit, they are sure to be punished and will immediately see the lack of profit or justice of such actions.

The most common types of punishment minority officers receive are poor work evaluations by supervisors, substantiated complaints against officers by citizens that would normally be unfounded, transfers to locations farthest from your residence, and assignment to mostly nights, weekends, and holidays. Numerous other undesirable assignments are used as forms of retaliation, such as waiting for extended periods of time at hospitals and psychiatric wards with prisoners and standing for extremely long periods of time at outside fixed posts in the middle of nowhere while the weather is often dismal. One of the most common reasons that many officers are targeted by police management is failing to comply with the department's unwritten quota policies to enter minority communities and proactively reach numerical goals for arrests and summonses during a period. The other most common reason is complaining against supervision or management about inappropriate conduct or behavior such as racial comments or sexual harassment. Intimidating officers to make arrests start at the top, from police executives and managers, who often claim the chief or commissioner wants numbers. Every chief, sheriff, or commissioner of every law enforcement agency or municipality will deny the fact that quotas exist.

It is quite unfortunate that many police personnel, including myself, had to record police supervisors and managers who often would talk about certain practices and demands from police officials above. These unwritten *police quotas* are the root of racial discrimination that affect minority communities across the country. Police departments continue to tell everyone that quotas don't exist, but hidden recordings of supervisors and commanders tell otherwise.

Recommendation:

Providing false information during any governmental hearings or administrative investigations while under oath is an arrest able offense. If someone is caught lying on audio or video footage, he or she can and will be prosecuted. This offense includes written documentation with signature affirmations. The DOJ needs to create a system like the Crime Stoppers program that allows law enforcement personnel to contact authorities anonymously and provide information about police misconduct and other activities relating to officers who violate the law or police policy.

In wake of the recent atrocious police shootings and the continuous controversial shooting deaths of African Americans by law enforcement, it is a complicated task to achieve an effective remedy for racial equality. America will not attain positive results when failing to acknowledge that there are multiple problems concerning law enforcement and African Americans and other people of color in America. The hiring of an African American police chief merely to disguise racism, sexual harassment, and other allegations of police discrimination and misconduct in law enforcement is common. While minorities in law enforcement continue to endure separate treatment and criteria for transfers, promotions, and special assignments, they are continuously denied the opportunities to speak out against the injustices brought upon them in fear of retaliation. Little relief is gained with unions, internal affairs, courts, and other police administrative hearings.

I recall a fellow officer telling me how he made a formal complaint to his superiors and in the process filed an Equal Employment Opportunity Commission (EEOC) complaint. The formal police complaint was quickly ruled unfounded with no in-house recourse. Unsurprisingly, the EEOC complaint was declared substantiated, but to no avail, because the officer was afraid of what might happen next. Nonetheless, the treatment of minorities in law enforcement continues to be intimidating and threatening, causing fear of reprisal, and there are administrative barriers that have been difficult to hold accountable and remove. It will be difficult to create any data relating to such abuses due to officers' fear of what will come if they cooperate. Minority officers complain that they still struggle with being treated equally to their white counter-parts and that it is common for them to be harassed or disciplined for expressing this. Given the hostile treatment that many minorities get from their peers and the public, especially in minority communities, they are often forced to comply and adapt to the *police culture*, which I like to call being "departmentalized." This is when police officers conform to and become established in the practices and customs of the *police culture*, affecting their performance, behavior, and identity. They abide by unorthodox and deceptive codes of conduct, following strategic plans of operations, practices, and acts that support and benefit the depart-ment's members. An example of one such code is how when an officer is assaulted by a subject, that individual will be physically attacked by the responding or trans-porting officers. One of the police's many mottos is, "We'll protect each other at any cost." Minority police officers tend to adapt consequently to police cultural pressure. Most minorities gain their peers' acceptance by adhering closely to the norms and behaviors of those they're surrounded by. Certain minority officers will try to be even more loyal, seeking promotion or to simply be left alone, and often act tougher than generally expected against other minority officers who do not act submissive to white authority or fail to follow the profession's norms, particularly when dealing with blacks and other minorities on the streets.

One of the main concerns regarding minorities in supervisory positions is the lack of authority. As I look back at my career in law enforcement, I can't recall a time when a black or minority supervisor ever took formal disciplinary action against any white employees. I asked my family members who have served in law enforcement along with other close associates, and none of them could recall such an incident either. Most white officers find it difficult to take orders from blacks and other minority supervisors. Some minorities fail to seek promotion because they refuse to conform to the abusive management culture.

Another area of concern is the development of an effective system that allows officers to provide information about police wrongdoing while maintaining anonymity. Police departments do not have policies that protect the identity of officers who report police misconduct. Anyone in a position of authority who witnessed wrongdoing or has knowledge of the same and takes no action is considered a participant and is a part of the problem. Minorities who are in supervisory or management positions, or those who seek such positions will turn a blind eye to internal misconduct such as racial discrimination or sexual harassment inflicted by upper management and those associated with it. Those minorities are often rewarded with promotions and transfers to desired units and divisions, and they are often exempt from abusive behaviors because of showing their loyalty and not interfering with illegal and inappropriate employment practices.

I recall my brother being told by his sergeant that he was not allowed to work with other minorities in his unit at the orders of the precinct commander. He told me that shortly after being told this, he entered the precinct while another black detective arrived. As they both walked down the hallway leading to their office, the supervisor approached my brother and said he needed to talk to him now. He brought my brother straight into his office and said, "Didn't I tell you not to ride with him?" My brother replied, "We arrived at the precinct at the same time and were walking to the office from the parking lot." The sergeant replied, "Oh, okay. Disregard."

The internal blue wall has existed within police departments since many departments began increasing the number of minorities in the workplace, and many of these officers were often treated unfairly. There is a need to have an outside agency investigate the treatment and conduct of those internally. Policing in general has created strong and powerful cliques within various divisions, units, sections, and platoons in almost all departments and at all levels in policing, including management; this is known as being one of the "*good ol' boys.*" Minorities in policing have often reported being abused by white superiors while being left out of training courses for opportunities to advance skills and be selected for specialized units, which are controlled by those *good ol' boys.* Being appointed as detectives or assigned to positions in specialized units are always given to white counterparts.

I cannot honestly recall a black supervisor taking disciplinary action against any white employees in my tenure as a police officer. Black supervisors would act against blacks and other minority officers regularly but not white officers. I've asked other minority officers the same, and they too could not recall such an incident. I'm sure there must be a contrast when disciplinary write-ups and dispositions by minority supervisors about white subordinates are compared to those with white supervisors and minority subordinates. Such a study can have interesting findings. There are also differences in how minority officers are disciplined compared to whites. A minority officer can commit an infraction against police rules and regulations and receive the maximum penalty. White officers will either get a slap on the wrist or not charged at all because they receive white privilege.

I recall being a coordinator and working an off-duty job at a restaurant. A police officer would be assigned work in uniform in the late-night hours, creating visibility and maintaining order. The police department has a written policy that officers who work off duty assignments must be paid by check, money order, or some other written note. Being paid by cash was strictly prohibited. Nearing the end of the officer's shift at the restaurant, the manager would open the register and take out the officer's total pay for that shift. The manager would then give the cash to the officer and instruct him or her to go the nearest convenience store and purchase a money order totaling the pay amount. The officer would purchase the money order and return to the manager, who would fill out the money order that documented the officer's pay for that day. Once a white male supervisor who had a personal vendetta against me for speaking out against inequality went to the restaurant, seeking whatever information he could find to use against me. He found out about the pay system at the restaurant, went back to the "good old boy" network, and told them that I and other officers were taking cash at an off-duty job. The matter was referred to the IAD, which later substantiated the claim. All the minority officers were charged with violating a minor infraction and received written reprimands. I immediately spoke with all the white officers who were assigned at the restaurant. None of the white officers were charged with any violations for working at the same restaurant following the same pay policy.

Shortly after being disciplined for allegedly taking cash money for working an off-duty job, I worked another off-duty job coordinated by a white male sergeant. Following the completion of the work tour, the coordinator paid me with cash money. I advised the coordinator that this is not a good idea, explaining that I was recently charged and disciplined for being paid with cash for working another off-duty job. The coordinator told me he knew about the incident and that it was personal. He said that what happened prior did not concern him and not to worry about accepting the money for working. He told me that the police administration went after me for speaking against them. Encountering this type of administrative behavior is not uncommon for minority officers who work in departments, particularly departments in southern states that do not acknowledge labor unions.

CHAPTER SIX

The Cover-Up

When we think of police corruption, the image that comes to mind is usually taking bribes from sources such as motorists or shanking down drug dealers. Corruption is much more complex and takes on many different forms, including the destruction of physical evidence. Obtaining confessions and taking witness statements is a crucial part of an attempt to obtain an accurate account of a series of events. Police officers are very aware of the evidence that prosecutors need to prove a case. When an incident has occurred and the confrontation between the police and citizens has failed to meet the criminal procedure law requirements for law enforcement, the need to gather conclusive evidence will then conflict with the constitutional rights of citizens. Very few citizen complaints are substantiated by internal police investigations, and litigations filed against police agencies in courts will continue to increase.

In recent times, police officers and law enforcement agencies across the country are attempting to conceal evidence of wrongdoing by members. Individuals who participate in such cover-ups operate within a systemic *police culture* that's common to all levels in policing. The IAD is a controversial division that is charged with policing the police. Internal affairs investigators process citizen complaints of police misconduct, investigating excessive or unnecessary force as well as *deadly force* by police officers. The IAD could be described as a unit that takes measures to deflect or minimize damage to the reputation of the department in the best interest of the chief of police. Most Police department IAD's work out of the chief's office and provide damage control through politics. It has become quite common that when a citizen captures a police incident on video, the footage contradicts the police department's account of events. It is no surprise that the information contained in investigative police reports is very contradictory to the video footage of actual incidents.

The country will continue to see an escalating number of videos and ongoing media coverage showing police brutality and other *excessive force* incidents, along with extremely high payouts in civil lawsuits from various police agencies. Many lawsuits to come will have a greater chance of success, due to the increasing number of recording devices. Detailed information is willfully omitted, while other series of events are fabricated to cover police actions. Legal action will also continue to rise due to continuous negligent police behavior.

Policing has created an economical commodity used as *broken windows*. The true *broken windows* concept was an effort by law enforcement to develop community support while combatting and controlling crime. Crime seems to thrive in low-income areas where buildings are boarded up and dilapidated, filled with trash and graffiti along with drugs and prostitution. These neighborhoods have an atmosphere of dis-order, creating tension and fear. Because of a lack of police presence, these neighborhoods send out crime promoting signals. Certain areas filled with criminal prone street people are the ones most likely to maintain a high level of crime. When police purposely withdraw from such communities, unaddressed disorderly behavior gives criminals crime promoting opportunities. Law-abiding citizens live in fear in these areas, and predatory criminals take advantage of such opportunities. When the police purposely and willfully abandon communities to create this type of high crime atmosphere, this type of police conduct is described as an act of extortion against the public, also known as *a work slowdown.* This act is also a retaliatory tactic used against citizens, communities, or politicians who oppose police officers in any fashion. Citizens need police cooperation at all levels. If the police are to reduce crime and successfully maintain order in communities, they must offer cooperation, support, and assistance to the citizens they serve. This tactic is commonly used by police unions when labor contract negotiations are on the agenda and during election year. An extremely high crime rate is certain to have a political impact on an incumbent who is not highly regarded by police officials. In the same manner that physicians and dentists practice preventive medicine and dentistry while providing care for their patients, the police should be providing care for the citizens they are sworn to protect and serve within all communities.

Broken windows' is a sanction against minorities with a financial framework implemented by police departments that use a proactive, aggressive law enforcement system developed to generate revenue. Jurisdictions have encouraged law enforcement officers to stop motorists and issue bogus tickets and to aggressively stop, detain, and issue summonses to persons particularly in low-income communities. Because this practice has generated an enormous amount of revenue, it has expanded to other areas within jurisdictions. The initial use of the *broken windows theory* was designed by law enforcement to target neighborhoods proactively utilizing quality of life enforcement, entering those low-income areas and enforcing minor offenses while looking for ways to stop criminals from victimizing these neighborhoods. It is believed that neighborhoods where minor offenses are not enforced create an environment that becomes a breeding ground for additional serious criminal activity and violence. Proponents of the *broken windows* theory first adopted this concept in the 1990s, using the NYPD's zero tolerance approach. A new practice that became common to police mangers was to utilize all their enforcement resources to produce economically while targeting crime, quotas, crime stats, and clearance rates, along with quality of life conditions within their areas of responsibility. The police began strictly enforcing laws about drinking in public, littering, public urination, graffiti, subway fare evasion, and so on.

Non-feasance is a strategy used by the police to elevate the crime rate very rapidly. Intentionally altering statistical data causes sudden changes in the crime rate. Altered statistical reporting practices also exaggerate criminal activities geographically. An increase in crime is often linked to politicians and policies, reflecting a police department's desire to show that crime is a problem resulting from specific changes. For example, to manipulate the wording of an incident that has occurred, police will record a vandalism and a larceny instead of a burglary to avoid counting it as a serious crime. The value of larcenies is underestimated, so the crime is not counted a more serious class crime. When police departments want to portray an increase in crime, a true and accurate account is defined and tallied, creating the desired spike in crime. Therefore, it is creativity that changes the overall crime rate, reflecting the way police report crime and the way crimes are recorded rather than any actual change in the amount or rate of crime.

The City of New York has consistently increased its revenue by aggressively enforcing state laws, city codes, and ordinances through quotas. The city's revenue projections are calculated through the police department's enforcement activities. For example, the DOJ's report concluded that police management and top city officials continuously work concert to coordinate aggressive enforcement while monitoring productivity to ensure revenue expectations are at a sustainable pace. Top law enforcement and city officials conduct weekly meetings highlighting revenue generating stats combined with aggressive crime enforcement strategies. These meetings are based upon the statistical analysis of revenue and enforcement activities within the various geographical areas defined as precincts. These meetings and the information shared are known as *comp-stat*, which is an abbreviation for complaint statistics. It was originally designed to address crime reduction, quality of life improvement, and personnel and resource management and accountability. During these meetings, personnel would discuss high profile cases, crime patterns, and future police enforcement activities.

The *comp-stat* meetings are a forum used by top city and police department officials to communicate with precinct commanders relating to the crime problems they face and statistical comparisons between them. This process allows top officials to monitor enforcement activities through arrests, summonses, parking tickets, towed vehicles, and other revenue generating initiatives. Precinct commanders who fail to meet productivity goals are tormented and ridiculed relentlessly during these gatherings. Precinct commanders then return to their respective precincts and demand supervisors to pressurize officers to undertake aggressive enforcement approaches to meet arrest and revenue generating expectations. Officers and detectives who produce well are given preferential treatment. Those who fail to meet productivity goals are reassigned to undesirable assignments, receive poor performance evaluations, are not considered for transfers or promotions, are forced to work holidays, weekends, and midnights, and are disciplined periodically through unsubstantiated complaints. Because of the pressure placed upon precinct commanders to not be spectacles during *comp-stat* meetings, overaggressive strategies in policing have fostered practices in law enforcement that are unconstitutional.

Statistical data show that programs like *stop-and-frisk* disproportionately target African Americans and Latinos. Furthermore, stops of minorities stem from racial bias and stereotypes. For example, blacks and other minorities encounter police during traffic stops and are viewed as being potentially engaged in criminal activity because they drive expensive vehicles. Doctors, lawyers, engineers, prosecutors, police officers, and many minorities from other professions all have informed me that being stopped and questioned by the police for no apparent reason is quite common. If you have tinted windows on your vehicle, the odds of being stopped increase dramatically. Police departments across the country fail to have a system in place to detect and hold officers accountable for misconduct relating to unconstitutional behavior or revenue generating activities.

The sudden dynamic reduction in crime, along with the successful revenue generating factors that has occurred in New York City piqued the curiosity of other police departments around the country, which soon followed suit. The *comp-stat system* is mirrored in cities such as Baltimore, Oakland, Philadelphia, Richmond, Los Angeles, Saint Louis, Washington, District of Columbia, and many others. Many of the police protests nationwide are attributed to the common unethical and unconstitutional law enforcement practices that are happening in the United States. Local law enforcement's aggressive policing motivated by top city officials to increase revenue have become normal police practices, resulting in a pattern of unconstitutional violations of individuals. Officers constantly violate the First, Fourth, and Eighth Amendments in stopping people without reasonable suspicion, arresting citizens without probable cause, and using unreasonable and *excessive force.* Officers often intimidate individuals and interfere with the rights of those who attempt to record police enforcement and activities. These continued unlawful police practices have elevated community mistrust, creating an atmosphere of tension during interactions. The *broken windows/comp-stat* concept of policing has led an overwhelming number of officers to conduct traffic stops, pedestrian stops, and arrests that violate citizens' constitutional rights. Officers will often break departmental rules, perhaps even violate the law, while making arrests and writing reports that falsely construct arrests that meet legal requirements. During the construction of such reports, officers and supervisors fabricate a series of events to justify stopping an individual or omit information that exonerates someone. Law enforcement officers are taught to always inject the phrase, "*I was in fear for my life*" when justifying any type of aggressive or *deadly force.*

The U.S. Constitution's Fourth Amendment provides limitations on police behavior against unreasonable searches and seizures. Minorities are often stopped and detained by police without articulable reasonable suspicion of criminal activity, leading to arrests without probable cause. Under the Fourth Amendment, stopping an individual, regardless of the amount of time, constitutes a deprivation of liberty if it fails to meet the legal require-ments. Many of these unlawful stops are attempts to discover whether a subject has a pending warrant on file while attempting to locate illegal contraband. Individuals who question officers about being stopped are often charged with disorderly conduct. This tactic is used to coerce individuals to comply with an officer's unlawful stop without objections. Any form of objection is construed as an aggressive resistance, even when the officer initiates aggressive behavior. Subjects who are stopped find themselves being aggressively threatened with acts of violent force combined with verbal abuse, and they suddenly become angry, afraid, and uncooperative due to a state of confusion and helplessness. Citizens refuse to cooperate when they know their rights have been violated.

Officers respond to these reactions by initiating aggressive and *excessive force*. They justify this behavior by stating that they are making a lawful arrest and they are in fear for their safety. The phrase *"in fear for my safety"* is a statement used by those in law enforcement to legally justify acts of physical force. Another catch phrase officers use when making traffic stops and to justify extracting minorities from vehicles is stating that due to fear for their safety, they are conducting *protective sweeps* of the interior of vehicles while checking for weapons. This type of police practice, which is an attempt to locate contraband or just ridicule and inconvenience someone who passively disagrees with an officer, is common. There are multiple incidences of use-of-force complaints against police departments across the country resulting from unlawful stops and arrests. When officers have abused their legal authority and stopped individuals without any suspicion that they have committed a crime, they exacerbate the confrontation by using *excessive force*.

Police encounters with minorities on the streets often occur randomly and without fulfilling any legal requirements.

Law enforcement officers frequently stop individuals who are behaving normally and when no complaints of their presence have been made. Police are not required to have sufficient evidence for an arrest to stop a person for brief questioning. Officers rapidly escalate confrontations with individuals they perceive to be not complying with their orders, resulting in *excessive force* and a resisting arrest charge. Numerous *excessive force* complaints result from individuals asking police officers what law they violated. Subjects are beaten for expressing their disagreement with officers while offering no aggressive behavior. Verbally expressing how you feel to police officers is seen as a form of disrespect to them and requires immediate punishment. People who verbally express their displeasure with police behavior, along with those who record police activities, are also subjected to police punishment. Police officers often violate individuals' rights when making arrests for what is interpreted by the officer as a disrespect or when someone verbalizes disapproval of an officer's language, behavior, or actions. This type of behavior by police is not only unconstitutional but in most cases criminal. Many officers use force not to offset or overcome a physical threat or attack but instead to inflict punishment, to send a message to others in the community that any form of behavior other than full submission will result in repeated physical aggression. *Excessive force* can be described as force that is greater than what a reasonable and prudent law enforcement officer would use under the circumstances. Such a level of force is unreasonable and unwarranted and is inconsistent with police training and the state's DCJS mandates.

Numerous individuals across the country are stopped by the police without reasonable suspicion and arrested without probable cause. When subjects refuse to stop or attempt to walk away, officers will almost always respond with *excessive force*. During these situations, officers will always convene to discuss an embellished series of events and articulate some fabricated reasonable suspicion that coincides with criminal activity. Upon the arrival of supervision or management, information is gathered and formatted to the officer's version. Serious criticism should be leveled at the fact that police investigate police. An unbiased or independent investigation will reveal vital information to any police related investigation because certain interrogation skills and evidence gathering techniques are essential to revealing information. Internal affairs and supervisory investigative reports are extremely controversial, since the investigation is being conducted from within. The IAD at times will assist police management when disciplinary action is brought against one of its own. For example, according to a Daily News article, *"Cover- Up"* (2014), an NYPD internal report was prepared following the death of Eric Garner that downplayed the seriousness of his conditions after the incident.

Eric Garner was tragically killed by NYPD officer Daniel Pantaleo while being arrested for allegedly peddling loose cigarettes. Selling loose cigarettes is the sale of individual cigarettes sold separately from the pack. Witnesses told investigators that Mr. Garner had just broken up a dispute when officers arrived and accused him of passing a cigarette to someone. A video recording shows Mr. Garner loudly denying that he was selling cigarettes. The recording shows Mr. Garner passively resisting arrest while refusing to comply with an officer's directions to submit his hands to be hand-cuffed. Suddenly, an officer in a green shirt puts Mr. Garner in a *chokehold*. According to the article, the use of *chokehold* is prohibited according to NYPD guidelines. Police officers are prohibited from using *chokehold* restraint tactics, which essentially choke individuals into unconsciousness to subdue them. The recording continues to the scene where you can hear Mr. Garner tell police that he could not breathe. Shortly thereafter, the video shows Mr. Garner on the ground for several minutes, apparently unconscious and unresponsive.

Two supervising officers failed to note the *chokehold* in the report. One supervisor claimed that Mr. Garner was not in great distress, while another supervisor informed investigators that Mr. Garner's condition did not seem serious and that he did not appear to get worse. Despite saying that Mr. Garner's condition did not seem serious, the supervisor also told investigators that she believed she heard Mr. Garner state that he was having difficulty breathing. The article states that a police source said cops found four full packs and one partial pack of Newport on Mr. Garner. Mr. Garner's death was ruled a homicide by the New York City Medical Examiner's Office. It is very unfortunate that someone in America can be killed for questioning police and speaking out about their behavior.

According to the article, Police Commissioner Bill Bratton said, "it appeared that Mr. Garner was put in a *chokehold*." The article mentions that the NYPD prohibited the use of *chokehold* in 1993 and that the city's independent watchdog has substantiated only ten *chokehold* cases filed against cops since 2009. Reports show that little to nothing happens to officers regarding these cases. In one of the cases from the Criminal Complaint Review Board (CCRB), the cop accused of putting a person in a *chokehold* lost up to ten vacation days.

You must ask yourself several questions about this incident. Was a crime committed, and if so, by whom—Mr. Garner or the police officer? Is there any evidence that can support a compelling argument for either side? What does the video show, and what does the medical examiner's report state? Was a thorough police investigation conducted, and what did it reveal? What about the crime scene? Did the police locate the possible witness who purchased the alleged cigarette from Mr. Garner? Was that cigarette ever recovered? Is there any surveillance or video footage showing when and where the alleged offense occurred? What evidence was or was not presented to the grand jury? Was evidence presented by the prosecutor? Was the officer allowed to present evidence on his own behalf? Did anyone speak on behalf of Mr. Garner? Was the grand jury process one-sided? Why do grand juries consider cases in a closed hearing in which only the prosecutor presents evidence? Does the criminal justice system need to reform the grand jury process?

Recommendation:

To help understand and determine the frequency of police related deaths and shootings, the DOJ should assume jurisdiction over all crime scenes while collecting evidence, data, and information from law enforcement agencies. The information provided will reveal patterns and trends in uses of *deadly force* that may be questionable as well as those that are justifiable. This is equivalent to how the National Transportation Safety Board (NTSB) oversees transportation accident investigations. The DOJ will create an independent U.S. government investigative division that is responsible for maintaining crime scene integrity and protecting human rights.

A published report has addressed questions surrounding footage from a security camera at a Burger King restaurant near police involved shooting. Laquan McDonald, a seventeen-year-old young boy, was shot sixteen times and killed by Chicago police on the night of October 20, 2014. Reports from the medical examiner revealed that nine of the shots struck the teenager in the back. The Burger King restaurant is located just south of the area where the shooting occurred. Following the shooting, Jay Darshane, the district manager for Burger King, reported that approximately four to five police officers arrived at the restaurant and requested to view the video. After being given the password to the equipment and examining the footage some three hours later, the officers left. The following day, an investigator from the Independent Police Review Authority (IPRA) arrived and asked to see the footage. It was at this time that eighty-six minutes of video, running from 9:13 p.m. to 10:39 p.m., were discovered missing. The shooting incident occurred at approximately 9:50 p.m. It was also reported that witnesses were forced away from the scene and given no opportunity to make statements or leave contact information for possible later interviews.

When conducting crime scene investigations, it is extremely vital that no one alters the scene. Evidence tampering can involve physical evidence as well as documents. Removing, repositioning, or adding new items within a crime scene is a form of evidence tampering. The main reason that individuals tamper with evidence is to change the perception of what occurred. When police officers respond to a crime scene, it is important that the area is secured and preserved in its original state. It is imperative that no one alters the scene until crime scene technicians can begin their thorough examination. It is not always possible to know whether physical evidence has been tampered with. This is also true if evidence has been destroyed. Evidence is anything, including statements that can support the truth of occurrences relating to a series of events. Evidence tampering can alter the course of court proceedings, which can lead to exonerations of guilty parties and punishment of the innocent.

Another criminal offense that can alter court proceedings is jury tampering. This occurs when a person attempts to influence members of a jury by means other than evidence and arguments presented in a court of law. These acts can include bribes or threats and can come from several sources, including family members, defendants, plaintiffs, or anyone with an interest in the case. Any juror who willfully participates in any such conduct and does not report it is subject to charges. Jury tampering can render a false verdict or mistrial and is extremely costly.

Witness tampering or attempting to interfere with the testimony of a witness, is another unlawful act. Witness testimony can be evidence in criminal and civil cases used by the prosecution, defendants, and plaintiffs. Interfering with the testimony of a witness is punishable by law and can obstruct the criminal prosecution of a case as well as interfere with civil cases. It is of utmost importance that the courts prosecute those who tamper with witnesses to protect the integrity of the justice system. Individuals who engage in witness tampering often try to coerce witnesses to alter their testimony to cover up illegal behavior or alter the truth. All testimony and physical evidence should be accessible to the media and the public, but so should all evidence that relates to the use of technology from police officer body cameras, to street cameras, and police surveillance videos, which allows accessibility to the public.

Finally, if it can be proven that a subject or police officer has engaged in prohibited behavior such as lying under oath or providing false statements and information to authorities, an arrest should occur. Regardless of the intent of the offender, he or she should be strictly liable for the consequences of such actions. Whether a police officer is involved in a cover-up to conceal a wrongdoing or an individual is lying to the police to support a known companion, both sides must be equally accountable.

Law enforcement agencies across the country must scrutinize their recruitment and training requirements. Future officers must be culturally sensitized to minority groups while possessing community-oriented problem-solving skills. The use of de-escalation tactics along with defusing techniques can enable responding officers to process fears stimulated by minority confrontations when responding to incidents that require decision making under highly charged conditions. Also, there must be guidelines governing the need for intervention by fellow officers to stop the use of *excessive force*. Those who fail to stop and cease such acts can be charged as accessories. Officers shall no longer be authorized to assault someone into compliance to affect an arrest. For example, an officer might say, "I will be tase you if you if you don't get out of the car," or the officer might punch someone in the face, saying, "Put your hands behind your back," while continuously and repeatedly striking them in the face. These acts of intimidation are not mandated by the DCJS or police training. When an officer fails to follow police policies and guidelines relating to the *use of force*, he or she should not be immune from the law.

Below is the New York State penal code relating to perjury. There are several other related offenses along with various degrees of penalties.

S 210.00 Perjury and related offenses; definitions of terms the following definitions are applicable to this article:

1. "Oath" includes an affirmation and every other mode authorized by law of attesting to the truth of that which is stated.

2. "Swear" means to state under oath.

3. "Testimony" means an oral statement made under oath in a proceeding before any court, body, agency, public servant or other person authorized by law to conduct such proceeding and to administer the oath or cause it to be administered.

4. "Oath required by law." An affidavit, deposition or other subscribed written instrument is one for which an "oath is required by law" when, absent an oath or swearing thereto, it does not or would not, according to statute or appropriate regulatory provisions, have legal efficacy in a court of law or before any public or governmental body, agency or public servant to whom it is or might be submited.

5. "Swear falsely." A person "swears falsely" when he intentionally makes a false statement which he does not believe to be true while (a) giving testimony, or (b) under oath in a subscribed written instrument. A false swearing in a subscribed written instrument shall not be deemed complete until the instrument is delivered by its subscriber, or by someone acting in his behalf, to another person with intent that it be uttered or published as true.

6."Attesting officer" means any notary public or other person authorized by law to administer oaths in connection with affidavits, depositions and other subscribed written instruments, and to certify that the subscriber of such an instrument has appeared before him and has sworn to the truth of the contents thereof.

7."Jurat" means a clause wherein an attesting officer certifies, among other matters, that the subscriber has appeared before him and sworn to the truth of the contents thereof.

GENERAL POLICE ORDER
CLEVELAND DIVISION OF POLICE

ORIGINAL EFFECTIVE DATE: March 1, 2002	REVISED DATE: August 8, 2014	NO. PAGES: 1 of 15	NUMBER: 2.1.01
SUBJECT: USE OF FORCE			
ASSOCIATED MANUAL: INSPECTION, INTERNAL AFFAIRS, EMPLOYEE ASSISTANCE UNITS	RELATED ORDERS: 1.1.22, 2.1.02, 2.1.03, 2.1.04, 2.1.06, and 4.1.10		
CHIEF OF POLICE: *Calvin D. Williams, Chief*			

Substantive charges are italicized

PURPOSE: To establish guidelines for members of the Cleveland Division of Police relative to the use of force. To provide direction and clarity in those instances when a person's actions require an appropriate use of force response.

POLICY: A respect for human life shall guide members in the use of force. Division members shall use only the force that is objectively reasonable to effectively bring an incident under control, while protecting the life of the member or others. **Excessive force is strictly prohibited.**

A member's responsibility is the protection of the public. Standards for the use of force are the same on-duty and off-duty. Members shall not use force that may injure bystanders or hostages, except to preserve life or prevent serious bodily injury. **Deadly force is never justified solely to protect property.** The use of force is not left to the unregulated discretion of the involved member. Use of force decisions are dictated by the actions of the resistant or combative person, *Division policy, proper tactics, and training.* Justification for the use of force is limited to the facts actually known or reasonably perceived by the member at the moment that force is used. Deadly force shall not be used to effect an arrest or prevent the escape of a person unless that person presents an imminent threat of death or serious bodily injury to members or others.

DEFINITIONS:

Force means the following actions by a member: any physical strike or instrumental contact with a person, or any significant physical contact that restricts movement of a person. The term includes, but is not limited to, the use of firearms, conducted electrical weapon (CEW - e.g. Taser), ASP, chemical spray, or hard empty hands, the taking of a person to the ground, or the deployment of a canine. The term does not include escorting or handcuffing a person, with no or minimal resistance.

PAGE: 2 of 15	SUBJECT: USE OF FORCE	GPO NUMBER: 2.1.01

Deadly Force is any action likely to cause death or serious physical injury. It may involve firearms, but also includes any force or instrument of force (e.g. vehicle, edged weapon) capable of causing death or serious injury. Deadly force includes firing at or in the direction of a person, head strikes with any hard object, *and any action that restricts the blood or oxygen flow through the neck.*

Less Lethal Force is any use of force other than that which is considered deadly force. Less Lethal force includes any affirmative physical action taken by a member to control a person. In addition to the less lethal force associated with the use of pepper spray, Taser (CEW) and the ASP baton, less lethal force **includes** the following:

1. Use of a member's body part(s) to strike a person;

2. Use of Division-issued intermediate weapons (See Section IV) deployed on approved body target areas (e.g. large muscle groups, not to include head strikes);

3. Use of joint manipulation and/or pressure point techniques;

4. Striking a person with an object (other than a firearm) that may be used as a weapon (i.e. portable radio or flashlight) on approved body target areas;

5. Wrestling with a person;

6. Actively holding/pinning a person against the ground or other fixed object;

7. Any deliberate force which causes injury to a person or causes a person to fall or collide with an object;

8. Use of a police canine that results in a dog bite; Purposeful physical contact by a police horse that results in injury;

9. Any other less lethal physical action required to control a resistant, combative, or violent person.

Objectively Reasonable Force is that level of force that is appropriate when analyzed from the perspective of a reasonable officer possessing the same information and faced with the same circumstances as the officer who actually used force. Objective reasonableness is not analyzed with hindsight, but will take into account, where appropriate, the fact that officers must make rapid decisions regarding the amount of force to use in tense, uncertain, and rapidly evolving situations. This policy guideline applies to all uses of force, not only the use of deadly force. Reference U.S. Supreme Court case Graham v. Conner (1989).

Intermediate Weapons are authorized instruments or devices approved and issued by the Division. These instruments or devices include, but are not limited to, the following: OC pepper-spray, the ASP baton, the Taser, and the Beanbag Shotgun.

Deadly Active (Category 1): A Deadly Active person is one who is presenting a deadly threat with a firearm, edged weapon, deadly ordnance, Taser/Conducted Electrical Weapon (reference GPO 2.1.06 Taser – Conducted Electrical Weapon), or any other instrument or substance capable of causing death or serious physical injury. Also included is an attempt to disarm the member, incapacitate the member or a life-threatening weaponless assault. The member objectively and reasonably perceives an imminent threat of death or serious physical injury to self or innocent others.

Actively Resistant/Self-Destructive Behavior (Category 2): An Actively Resistant person is one who takes an offensive or a physically resistant action. These actions can take the form of the person standing at the ready and menacing with an object, device, or material capable of inflicting serious injury; the person using bodily force such as punching, striking, scratching, grabbing/holding; the person using active physical resistance to custody or presenting an imminent biohazard threat such as spitting or throwing a biohazard at the member or attempt of same. Also in this category: evading custody (escape), destroying evidence, or attempting to harm self (ingesting narcotics, suicide attempt), making explicit verbal threats to cause injury to the member or others present and which the member reasonably believes the person will carry out that threat. The member objectively and reasonably perceives an actual or imminent threat to self, others or evidence. In the interest of officer safety, members shall be particularly vigilant of persons presenting physical cues of an imminent attack (yawning with outstretched arms, glancing around assessing the environment, staring at the officer's duty belt, balling fists, shifting their body into a fighting stance ...).

Passively Resistant (Category 3): A Passively Resistant person is one who fails to follow voice commands. A Passively Resistant person may be verbally abusive using non-threatening language. A Passively Resistant person is also any person who resists arrest simply by passively refusing to comply as directed (dead weight). The police member does not objectively and reasonably perceive an imminent physical threat.

PROCEDURES:

I. Members who are present at the scene of a police-involved use of force are not relieved of the obligation to ensure that the use of force complies with the requirements of the law; and, in the instance of a Cleveland police officer, adherence to Divisional rules, policy, and training. Members of the Division of Police have a duty to act if the use of force against a person by any law enforcement officer clearly becomes excessive or objectively unreasonable.

PAGE	SUBJECT	GPO NUMBER
4 of 15	USE OF FORCE	2.1.01

A.   Members shall factor into their response their ability to deescalate the use of force. The witnessing member's response may range from physical intervention, to voice commands, to appropriate after-action notification. If reasonably able to do so, the member shall intervene physically to deescalate the application of force. The member shall also:

    1.   If reasonably able to do so, take *protective* custody of the person *being subjected to* the objectively unreasonable force.

    2.   Ensure that medical care is provided as needed.

    3.   In all cases, report witnessed suspected excessive use of force to the next non-involved supervisor in their chain of command before reporting off duty, and documenting same in their daily duty report and a Form-1 to the next non-involved supervisor in their chain of command.

B.   Supervisors shall investigate all reports of alleged excessive force brought to their attention and take action as appropriate. Supervisors shall in all such instances promptly make their superior aware of the allegation and proposed action. The supervisor investigating the allegation of excessive force shall contact the *Commander of the Bureau of Integrity Control* and advise same of the allegation. At this point, the *Commander of the Bureau of Integrity Control* may at his/her discretion take over the investigation of the allegation.

II.   Officers shall be trained and tested yearly on the law and Division policy regarding the use of force, appropriate methods to effect arrests, and the apprehension of fleeing persons. The Division mandates strict knowledge and compliance with this order. Immediate supervisors are responsible for clarifying misunderstandings associated with this order.

III.   Force Level

A.   Members shall first attempt verbal persuasion tactics and warnings to gain *the person's* cooperation. If verbal persuasion and warnings do not gain compliance, *members* shall obtain assistance to gain the *person*'s cooperation through a show of force. If a show of force does not gain compliance, the *member* shall use physical holds.

B.   Members shall determine the level of force necessary to protect themselves or others, or gain compliance from combative, resistant, or violent persons. Members shall consider alternative tactics to the use of force, which include, but are not limited to:

Police Brutality Matters

1.   Concealment and/or cover.

2.   Voice commands and other verbal attempts to deescalate the situation.

3.   *Use of a Crisis Intervention Team (CIT) officer, if available.*

4.   Show of force (i.e. multiple officers, display of weapons).

5.   *Judiciously allow time and/or opportunity for a person to regain self-control or cease struggling/resisting, when their actions do not immediately threaten the safety of themselves or others.*

C.   Action-Response

1.   Members are prepared with knowledge of laws, proper training in use of force decision-making, proper training and accountability to high ethical standards, and an understanding of Division directives. The member's response shall be judged strictly on what objectively reasonable is based on the totality of circumstances and all facts known or reasonably perceived by the member at the moment that a force response is employed.

2.   Members shall be guided by the person's actions as they fall into three general categories: **Deadly Active (Category 1)**, **Actively Resistant/Self-Destructive Behavior (Category 2)**, and **Passively Resistant (Category 3)**. Members shall refer to their training and the Use of Force *policy (GPOs and attachments)* for guidance in tailoring the appropriate response as prompted by the person's actions.

D.   Members shall consider the following member/person factors when choosing an Action-Response:

1.   Age

2.   Gender

3.   Body size

4.   Skill level

5.   Number of persons and number of members

6.   Relative strength of the person and member

7.   Known or apparent medical condition

PAGE: 6 of 15	SUBJECT: USE OF FORCE	GPO NUMBER: 2.1.01

8.   Known or apparent drug/alcohol usage

E.   Special circumstances unique to each situation involving use of force:

    1.   Weapon proximity

    2.   Injury or exhaustion

    3.   Position (e.g., being on the ground)

    4.   Distance from the person

    5.   Special knowledge or training

    6.   Availability of other options

    7.   Environmental conditions

    8.   The person presents threat of a bio-hazard (saliva, blood, other body fluids) by way of spitting or throwing the bio-hazard at a member.

    9.   Degree to which the person is already restrained (handcuffed, physically controlled by others, or whose mobility has been otherwise severely compromised).

IV.   Intermediate Weapons

    A.   Members who successfully complete mandated training and meet the Division's proficiency standards are issued and required to carry intermediate weapons on duty and while engaged in secondary employment. Members who are Taser, ASP, and OC Spray qualified shall carry the Taser and at least one other intermediate weapon as so qualified. If not Taser qualified, members *shall* carry both the ASP and OC Spray as so qualified.

    B.   Members shall carry and use only those intermediate weapon holsters/carriers furnished by the Division or specifically authorized by the Chief of Police.

    C.   *Intermediate weapons shall not be used on passively resistant persons.*

    D.   Members may draw, display, point or threaten to use intermediate weapons if they fear for their safety or the safety of others, or to gain compliance from a resistant, combative, or violent person.

    E.   Batons/Hard Objects Used as a Weapon.

PAGE 7 of 15	SUBJECT: USE OF FORCE	DPO NUMBER: 2.1.01

1. The Division authorizes a member to use an *ASP* baton while on duty or working secondary employment. Absent exigent circumstances, the Division prohibits the use of non-traditional weapons/hard objects to gain compliance from resistant, combative, or violent person(s).

2. The "Riot Baton" is authorized only during field force deployment.

3. When a member uses the ASP baton, Riot Baton, or any hard object/non-traditional weapon, medical personnel shall examine the person (i.e. EMS, Emergency Room).

4. Photographs of the area struck by an ASP baton, Riot Baton, or any hard object/non-traditional weapon shall be taken and be made part of the investigative packet.

F. Oleoresin Capsicum "OC" Spray

1. If feasible, members shall provide a loud verbal warning before OC spray is used.

2. Members shall not use OC spray on women known or believed to be pregnant.

3. *Members shall not use OC spray on persons with a known respiratory condition unless it is an extreme and articulable situation.*

4. If OC spray is used on a juvenile, elderly, pregnant, physically disabled person, or a suspected mentally ill person, they shall be transported to the nearest hospital for treatment.

5. Members shall assist bystanders who come into contact with OC discharges. If an injury occurs or medical attention is required, the member shall complete an Injury to Person/Accidental/OC Spray Record Management System (RMS) report and ensure that a copy of it is forwarded through the chain of command to the Inspection Unit.

6. If a person does not comply after two one-second bursts of OC that successfully reach the target, members shall discontinue use.

7. When control is established at the scene, the member shall make a reasonable effort to relieve the person's OC discomfort. Members shall wash OC from the person's eyes as soon as possible at the scene, the booking location, or a hospital.

8. Immediately transport persons for emergency medical care if:

   a. Symptoms, other than mild, last beyond 45 minutes.

   b. The person has difficulty breathing or loses consciousness.

   c. The member believes that the person needs medical attention, regardless if the person requests it or not.

   d. The member becomes aware of a medical condition (bronchitis, heart ailment, emphysema, etc.) that OC spray may aggravate.

9. Members shall carefully handle a person's clothing that has come in contact with OC spray to avoid OC contact themselves.

10. The use of OC on a person attempting to swallow evidence or contraband is permitted when all the following criteria have been met:

   a. There is a clear indication that the object or substance in the person's mouth is contraband.

   b. There are exigent circumstances such as the imminent destruction of evidence or medical emergency.

   c. The person has refused to comply with the member's verbal command to spit out any contraband.

   d. OC use is not prohibited by another section of this order.

G. *Taser*

   1. *Taser use shall comply with General Police Order 2.1.06 Taser.*

   2. *When the Taser is used a Taser download shall be completed by a supervisor or a Bureau of Integrity Control investigator.*

V. *Use of Less Lethal Force (ULLF)*

   A. When force is used, whether or not an injury occurs (whether on-duty, off-duty, or secondary employment) members shall promptly request a supervisor to respond to the scene. Members shall obtain necessary medical assistance for persons appearing to be injured or complaining of injury. An on-duty superior officer from the district in which the incident occurs shall investigate off-duty/secondary employment members' use of force. Supervisors who

PAGE:	SUBJECT:		GPO NUMBER:
9 of 15		USE OF FORCE	2.1.01

observe, participate in, authorize, or are otherwise involved in the use of force shall not assume investigative responsibilities of the incident.

B. In cases where members assigned to multi-agency units or task forces are involved in a *ULLF* incident, the supervisor who is next in the chain of command that did **not** observe, participate in, authorize, or otherwise was involved shall assume investigative responsibilities of the *ULLF*.

C. When less lethal force is used, members shall complete a RMS report with "Police Intervention" in the title. One such titled report is sufficient to cover all members involved in a single incident of ULLF as long as that report contains all the information in the narrative section that accounts for each member's ULLF actions.

   1. The member completing the RMS report shall include the notation "Use of Less Lethal Force report completed" in that narrative.

   2. The member completing the RMS report shall identify within it all members who used force during the incident *and identifiable witnesses; including civilians, members of other agencies, and members of the Division.*

D. The member completing the RMS report shall complete the ULLF report (Attachment A) and the additional members involved (Attachment B) as necessary. *One ULLF report (4 pages) shall be completed for each person force was used against.* The reporting member shall ensure that all the involved members' actions are noted on the ULLF report.

   1. Failed attempts at force, such as the missed thrust of a punch, the missed swing of an ASP, or a failed takedown attempt, also need to be documented in the ULLF report as they are indicative of the officer's intentions. Officers shall ensure that these failed attempts at force are clearly described in the narrative of the RMS report.

   2. When completing the Action Response section (page 2) of the ULLF report, members shall check <u>all</u> boxes in <u>all</u> categories indicating <u>all</u> person and member actions as appropriate. It is possible that a use of force event may require that multiple boxes be checked in all three categories for both the person and the member.

   3. Before reporting off duty, the member completing the RMS report shall:

a. Submit the original RMS and ULLF reports to the investigating supervisor. The supervisor shall sign the reports after having checked them for accuracy and completeness.

b. Fax the supervisor-signed Police Intervention RMS and ULLF reports *(all 4 pages)* to the Record Intake/Review Unit <u>and</u> to the Inspection Unit.

c. Forward the original supervisor-signed RMS report *and a copy of the ULLF report* to the district/bureau Commander's Office for later forwarding to Record Intake/Review Unit.

4. The member shall return a copy of the RMS report and the original ULLF report and other documents to the investigating supervisor for the completion of the investigation and additional endorsements in the chain of command and for final forwarding to the Chief's Office.

E. Supervisors notified of the ULLF shall immediately respond to the scene and conduct an objective, impartial, complete investigation to include a review of all known relevant video and audio evidence.

1. Supervisors shall ensure that medical care has been provided for as needed. If EMS is not conveying the prisoner, the supervisor shall judiciously consider if it is appropriate to have members who were involved in that use of force to also handle the transport of that prisoner to a medical facility. <u>Given the totality of the circumstances of the use of force and available staffing</u>, the supervisor may assign the prisoner transport to other non-involved members.

2. *The supervisor handling the ULLF investigation shall require all members that were on scene just prior to, during, or immediately after the ULLF to complete a Form-1 that details any actions of the member and what the member observed and heard. When determining if a member should complete a Form-1, the supervisor shall take into account that it is better to complete a Form-1 than not.*

3. The supervisor handling the initial ULLF investigation shall prepare an investigative packet. *One packet shall be created for each person that force was used against. Each packet shall include:*

   a. *A supervisor's investigative Form-1. When there are multiple persons involved in a single incident, one supervisor's investigative Form-1 shall be completed and a copy included with each investigative packet. The Form-1 shall include:*

1. A Synopsis of the incident and an evaluation of the ULLF addressing whether or not the force was appropriate and in compliance with Division rules and procedures.

2. *The use of proper names instead of pronouns (e.g. he, she, they) or RMS report type references (e.g. offender, suspect, victim).*

3. *Interviews of the person and all available witnesses.*

4. *No blanket statements such as "all officers/witnesses agree." Instead, supervisors shall reference individual statements from the RMS report, ULLF report, or interviews and attribute them to the source.*

b. Copies of associated RMS and accident reports.

c. The member's original ULLF report *(4 pages)* containing the supervisor's appropriate endorsements/comments and other completed sections.

d. *Form-1s from all members that were on scene just prior to, during, and immediately after the ULLF.*

e. Photographs *of the person and* any injuries to members or witnesses; as well as photos of areas on the person's body where an officer applied force, <u>regardless if there is visible injury or not</u>. The head and face area shall be included even though these areas will be photographed during booking.

f. Copies of any records of medical treatment.

g. *Hard copies of Taser download data labeled with the involved officer's name and badge number.*

h. Copy of any photographic or video evidence available. A non-exhaustive list of sources of such evidence include the Bureau of Homeland Services (Jail and Division of Police buildings), the Aviation Unit, in-car mobile video recording (MVR) video, video or still photographs from an officer's personal electronic device, and private source video such as security system recordings utilized by businesses and residences. *The supervisor's Form-I should note the location (e.g. time, counter, or frame) of the pertinent ULLF action.*

    i.   If the ULLF is the result of a secondary employment action, determine if the member had approval to work said secondary employment. The investigating supervisor shall contact the Personnel Unit to determine the member's secondary employment status, or if unable to do so during normal business hours, request that the day shift administrative supervisor handle this task. This task may be handled via e-mail.

    j.   *For tracking purposes, the person's name and the RMS number shall be on all documents, photos, and/or videos in the packet.*

    4.   The investigating supervisor shall within 7 calendar days of the incident forward the packet through their chain of command. Supervisors in the chain of command shall each have 7 calendar days to review and assess the force used to determine if it is in compliance with Division rules and procedures. If an investigative review cannot be completed within the 7 day period, the investigative supervisor shall complete a Form-1 stating the reason for the delay and request an additional 7 days, and forward same through the chain of command. Each subsequent delay requires a new Form-1.

F.   The commander's office shall ensure that the investigative packet is complete and accurate, placed in an envelope marked Use of Less Lethal Force (separate from the daily inter-office mail), and forwarded through the chain of the command to the Deputy Chief in that investigating supervisor's chain of command.

G.   After review and endorsement, the Deputy Chief shall forward the investigative packet (with their recommendation) to the Chief of Police.

H.   *ULLF investigation packets shall not be separated during the review and endorsement process. If a portion of the packet needs correction or clarification the entire investigative packet shall be returned.*

I.   The Inspection Unit shall collect all ULLF reports that are faxed to them and *enter them* into a database for tracking purposes and statistical analysis.

PAGE	SUBJECT:	GPO NUMBER:
13 of 15	USE OF FORCE	2.1.01

J.   Officers involved in an off-duty police action involving a ULLF outside the City of Cleveland shall:

    1.   When safely able to do so, immediately notify Communications Control Section (CCS) of the incident and when the member is scheduled or expected to return to duty. CCS shall notify the member's commander.

    2.   Upon return to duty, the member shall:

        a.   Notify their immediate supervisor of the incident.

        b.   Complete an RMS report titled: "Police Intervention / Outside Cleveland." The 'INCIDENT" box shall be checked. **Do not** check the "OFFENSE" box and **do not** list any of the offenses or code numbers. The RMS report shall contain the following information about the incident: date, time, location, and jurisdiction. No details of the incident are to be included in the RMS report. The RMS report and number are for **tracking and documentation only**.

        c.   Complete a ULLF report (Attachment A) as described in this order.

        d.   Complete a Form-1 describing the incident in detail similar to a ULLF RMS report for an incident occurring inside Cleveland.

        e.   Obtain a copy of the incident report from the reporting agency.

    3.   Provide all the materials described here to their immediate supervisor to complete a ULLF investigation as described in this order.

VI.   Use of Deadly Force/Firearms

    A.   Officers who meet the Division's requirements and demonstrate proper proficiency shall be allowed to carry firearms.

    B.   Officers shall carry and use only those weapons, holsters, and ammunition furnished by the City of Cleveland or authorized by the Chief of Police.

    C.   Officers may draw, display, or point a weapon if they fear for their own safety or the safety of others.

Joseph J. Ested

D. *Officers shall not discharge any firearm at or from a moving vehicle unless deadly force is being used against the police officer or another person present by means other than the moving vehicle.*

E. Officers shall not fire warning shots.

VII. Investigation of Deadly Force

    A. Officers shall:

        1. Immediately notify their superior.

        2. Obtain necessary medical assistance for persons who appear to be injured or complain of injury.

        3. Always maintain their firearm immediately ready for use (fully loaded and functional), especially while still engaged in an evolving, unresolved, or threatening situation.

        4. Be reminded that their firearm is evidence after a use of deadly force incident, and therefore shall not unnecessarily manipulate, handle or clean their firearm prior to turning over custody of same to the UDFIT OIC or UDFIT OIC's designee. This directive shall never prevent an officer from clearing a malfunction or reloading while still engaged in an evolving, unresolved, or threatening situation. For safety reasons, officers shall make the UDFIT OIC or designee aware of their firearm's condition if it is in any condition other than fully functional.

        5. Be immediately removed from street duty, and assigned temporarily to non-sensitive work, if they cause death or injury.

        6. Complete a post-traumatic stress incident debriefing program if they cause death or injury, and not return to street duty until so ordered by the Chief of Police.

    B. Sector Supervisors shall:

        1. Immediately respond to the scene and take control.

        2. Advise the CCS to notify UDFIT immediately upon learning there has been a use of deadly force incident by a police officer or any use of force by a Cleveland police officer resulting in serious injury to another person or the officer. The supervisor shall direct the CCS to first notify UDFIT before any other notifications are made (i.e. Labor

PAGE: 15 of 15	SUBJECT: USE OF FORCE	GPO NUMBER: 2.1.01

Unions of involved members, Employee Assistance Unit, and Office of Professional Standards). These units perform a support function to UDFIT.

3. Ensure that medical care has been provided for as needed.

4. Ensure that witnesses have been identified and separated.

5. Ensure that involved officers have been identified and separated. Due care shall be taken that each separated officer is NOT isolated and is in the company of a non-involved person at all times.

6. Take a firearm into custody when the officer involved has suffered an injury or other trauma/incapacitation up until such time that it can be transferred to the custody of UDFIT.

7. Ensure that the crime scene is secure and that an officer is assigned responsibility for maintaining the crime scene and the Crime Scene Entry Log.

8. Confer with the OIC of UDFIT and ensure that all related RMS reports are generated as required.

C. A Crime Scene and Records Unit detective shall identify, photograph, collect, log, and secure all evidence at a Use of Deadly Force scene.

D. Immediately following the initial on-scene investigation, the involved officer(s) shall appear at the Homicide Unit. UDFIT may direct the involved officer(s) to transfer to the Homicide Unit custody of their body armor, uniform, leather gear, equipment, or other items as needed.

E. Uses of Less Lethal Force that are immediately related to or occur concurrently with a Use of Deadly Force shall be handled by UDFIT. This is applicable in incidents when an officer employed both less lethal and deadly force, as well as to officers who employed only less lethal force during the same deadly force incident.

CDW/jeh
Policy & Procedures Unit
Attachments (ULLF - Forms A & B)

CHAPTER SEVEN

Tricks of the Trade

In recent years, the public has become genuinely concerned about police brutality. A great deal of public interest has focused on police behavior and account- tability. In this chapter, I will explain the clever ways police departments across the country are operating and per- forming police activities that are especially dishonest and unfair to citizens of all kinds, particularly minorities. These ingenious techniques that are used in policing are unknown by all who are not part of the *police culture*. These clever methods help police officers do their job. This chapter is intended to expose these ingenious techniques by recognizing the harms caused by these law enforcement practices. These acts can be better understood, and a system put in place to deter them.

The Constitution continues to play a critical role in the development of the criminal procedure laws used in the criminal justice system. The Bill of Rights was structured to prevent government from infringing on the personal freedom of citizens. The Bill of Rights was adopted to protect individual liberties from being abused by the federal government, but unfortunately, it does not apply to the actions of state and local governments. The mandate that govern criminal procedure are required by several amendments of the U.S. Constitution and Bill of Rights. The Fourth and Eighth Amendments furnish the basis for the system of criminal procedure that needs to be closely scrutinized to help define and control the limits of governmental action against minorities on state and local levels.

The Fourth Amendment to the U.S. Constitution provides some major limits on police behavior. It states the following:

> The right of the people to be secure in their persons, houses, papers, and effects, against unreasonable searches and seizures, shall not be violated, and no warrants shall issue, but upon probable cause, supported by oath or affirmation, and particularly describing the place to be searched, and the persons or things to be seized.

The Fourth Amendment is especially important for the criminal justice system because it controls law enforcement. Such regulations mean that police officers cannot indiscriminately use their authority to stop subjects to investigate a possible crime or arrest a suspect unless either or both actions are justified by the law and the facts and circumstances dictate it. Stopping, questioning, or searching individuals without legal justification represents a serious violation of the Fourth Amendment. The right to privacy is not unlimited but is protected until certain legal requirements are met. Police can search and seize individuals or evidence when sufficient evidence is presented to a judge or magistrate. Police can also legally search someone without a warrant when that person has been lawfully arrested. Because the police are constantly involved with stopping citizens, the Fourth Amendment is one of the most critical issues to be scrutinized. If people are accused of a crime and they believe that they were illegally stopped, searched, or arrested, they can have their attorneys file a motion to suppress. Federal courts need to formulate and enforce laws against law enforcement officers that knowingly stop individuals or seize evidence in violation of a person's Fourth Amendment rights. The U.S. Supreme Court also needs to extend Fourth Amendment protection against prosecutors who willfully withhold evidence that can prove someone's innocence.

Former Republican Mayor Rudy Giuliani hired William Bratton as his police commissioner, who implemented the *broken windows* style of policing in New York City. The positive implementation of the *broken windows theory* was to correct urban disorder and vandalism leading to additional criminal activity and violent anti-social behavior. This theory, implemented through strategic policing with lawful methods, was designed to maintain a well-ordered condition while monitoring urban areas. Police created methods of stopping individuals to deter disorder and property crimes, which tend to escalate into more serious criminal activities. It is extremely un-fortunate that the NYPD's policies were put in place to bogusly stop individuals across the city to raise revenue. These practices not only violated the individuals' constitut-ional rights but created an atmosphere of tension between police and all types of citizens. Failure to enact police reform and accountability is detrimental to restoring trust in law enforcement.

The NYPD's *stop-and-frisk* practices are found in the New York State's Criminal Procedure Law, which states this:

S140.50 Temporary questioning of persons in public places; search for weapons:

1. In addition to the authority provided by this article for making an arrest without a warrant, a police officer may stop a person in a public place located within the geographical area of such officer's employment when he reasonably suspects that such person is committing, has committed or is about to commit either (a) a felony or (b) a misdemeanor defined in the penal law, and may demand of him his name, address and an explanation of his conduct.

2. Any person who is a peace officer and who provides security services for any court of the unified court system may stop a person in or about the courthouse to which he is assigned when he reasonably suspects that such person is committing, has committed or is about to commit either (a) a felony or (b) a misdemeanor defined in the penal law, and may demand of him his name, address and an explanation of his conduct.

3. When upon stopping a person under circumstances prescribed in subdivisions one and two, a police officer or court officer, as the case may be, reasonably suspects that he is in danger of physical injury, he may search such person for a deadly

weapon or any instrument, article or substance readily capable of causing serious physical injury and of a sort not ordinarily carried in public places by law-abiding persons. If he finds such a weapon or instrument, or any other property possession of which he reasonably believes may constitute the commission of a crime, he may take it and keep it until the completion of the questioning, at which time he shall either return it, if lawfully possessed, or arrest such person.

4. In cities with a population of one million or more, information that establishes the personal identity of an individual who has been stopped, questioned and/or frisked by a police officer or peace officer, such as the name, address or social security number of such person, shall not be recorded in a computerized or electronic database if that individual is released without further legal action; provided, however, that this subdivision shall not prohibit police officers or peace officers from including in a computerized or electronic database generic characteristics of an individual, such as race and gender, who has been stopped, questioned and/or frisked by a police officer or peace officer.

The NYPD has begun implementing a new process that provides individuals who are stopped with an explanation for the stop along with a *stop-encounter card*. A receipt is supposed to ensure citizens who are stopped receive accurate information identifying the officer who initiated the stop along with information justifying the encounter. This new initiative is a way of documenting stops that officers justify a reason for obtaining information. This type of stop requires some type of suspicious criminal activity but is also a tool used to gather information.

Pictured herein is the new NYPD receipt that police officers will be required to issue to citizens who are questioned and frisked during street stops. There are seven boxes on the receipt that are alleged factors that contribute to the officer's suspicion and constitute a stop.

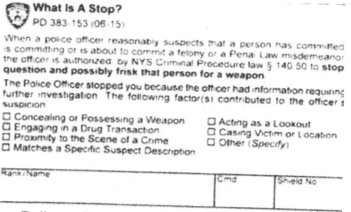

Police officers are permitted by law to search individuals without a search warrant incident to a lawful arrest. Another important exception to the rule of requiring a search warrant is the *stop-and-frisk* process. Police officers are not required to have sufficient evidence for an arrest to stop, question, and frisk. The NYS criminal procedure law authorizes the *stop-and-frisk* procedure using standards established by the Supreme Court in the case of *Terry v. Ohio (1968)*. Police officers are lawfully allowed to stop, question, and frisk subjects while investigating suspicious behavior without having to meet any probable cause standards. The *stop-and-frisk* policies are based primarily on the statements of the police that determine whether suspicious conduct occurred. The act of frisking should be limited to instances in which a police officer determines that his or her safety is in danger. However, the process has become a tool used to conduct exploratory searches and harass minority citizens. Police officers are constantly seizing contraband detected by touch during protective pat-down searches done to locate illegal items.

The *stop-and-frisk* process relating to a police officer's articulation of suspicious behavior needs to be thoroughly and comprehensively scrutinized. Police officers frequently stop individuals who may be in high crime areas without reasonable suspicion. What is reasonable suspicion? Reasonable suspicion should be formed based on specific and articulable facts that, when taken together with rational inferences from those facts, would cause a reasonably prudent person in the circumstances to believe that the person he or she is dealing with has committed, is committing, or is about to commit a felony. Random stops, also known as *sweeps* are a practice in which a group of officers jump out of a police car onto groups of minorities that are congergated in an area. Officers begin conducting searches of individuals while running warrant checks of names through databases such as the NCIC, hoping to get a positive hit while searching for drugs and contraband.

I recall my brother telling me the story of when he drove into a bogus police checkpoint conducted by two NYPD offices in the borough of Queens. This setup was at the off ramp of the Van Wyck Expressway at the southbound Rockaway Boulevard exit. Upon exiting the expressway, he was stopped by an officer who directed him to drive approximately one hundred feet to the second officer, where he was checked for warrants and a license suspension. When he pulled over to the side of the road, the officer asked him if he had ever had a New York driver's license. The vehicle he was operating had Virginia license plates. He explained that he had been a New York City correctional officer in the late 1980s and moved to Virginia, changing his license, upon becoming a police officer. The officer said people often go to other states to obtain valid driver licenses after becoming suspended in New York. He said, "You'd be surprised how many people we catch like this." As the officer walked a short distance away to transmit his information via radio, my brother began looking around the area, where numerous individuals were stopped and sitting in their cars waiting to be released. All of them were minority men and women who had vehicles with out-of-state license plates. During this time, several vehicles containing white motorists with license plates from other states drove through the area without incident. This type of stop is very common and should be video recorded by watch groups and brought to the attention of the American Civil Liberties Union (ACLU) and other organizations that protect the rights of others.

Following *comp-stat* meetings, many of the precinct commanders immediately communicate to division and unit commanders the need to increase traffic summonses and arrests because of the low productivity numbers that were exposed during the meetings. Police managers communicate to officers that they should focus on high quotas not only to raise the arrest stats higher but also to misclassify serious crimes reported to reflect a lower crime rate.

It was in the summer of 2009 when I met with my brother and we went to his new house in Far Rockaway, New York. The house was in the final stages of being completely renovated. Upon arriving at the front of the house, we noticed that several miscellaneous items and other debris were in the front yard and the front window on the ground level was broken. The front door was closed but unlocked as we entered. Numerous items were on the floor throughout the residence, and bedroom doors and walls were also vandalized. The police were called to take a report of a burglary. Upon the arrival of the officers, they walked throughout the house examining the point of entry as well as the damages. They advised my brother that the damages were not that bad and that they've seen worse. They also asked him if anything was stolen. He told them that several items were missing but he wasn't sure what else had been taken at this time since so many items had been moved from their original locations. One of the officers asked my brother why he was making a report; this was followed by a comment suggesting that my brother may be attempting to file a false insurance claim. My brother explained to the officers that the contractor was still working on the house and would need a copy of the report to replace the damage that had occurred. The officers stated that they would file the report as a vandalism and a larceny instead of an actual burglary. They explained that their precinct commander would become angry if they recorded a higher crime occurrence instead of a lower-class crime.

Law enforcement agencies across the country tabulate the number of index crimes that are recorded by the Federal Bureau of Investigations (FBI), and this is used to determine a locality's crime rate. The Uniform Crime Report (UCR), which is prepared by the FBI, is the best known and most widely cited source of criminal statistics. Index I Crimes such as murder, non-negligent manslaughter, rape, robbery, aggravated assault, burglary, grand larceny, arson, and motor vehicle theft are collected. For example, changing a report that is classified as a felony from aggravated assault to a report that is classified as a misdemeanor assault is a purposeful method used to project an artificial drop in the crime rate. Because police rebel against change, it causes a rebellious movement by the police. Police create changes in reporting crime that alters the crime rate. An increase in the crime rate will reflect the desire of a police department to show it is dissatisfied with the political involvement and all those who respond to community pressures and interest groups alike. Therefore, the overall crime rate will reflect the way the police are now suddenly recording incidents rather than any actual change in the amount or rate of crime. As in the example mentioned earlier, the actual aggregated assault would be recorded correctly rather than as the misclassified downgrade reflecting a misdemeanor assault. All proactive initiatives and preventive patrol tactics have been abandoned to promote criminal opportunities throughout communities.

The tragic incident of 9/11 has made the United States aware of the threat that terrorism presents to the public. The Oklahoma City bombing has made the country aware of the threat domestic terrorism presents to the public as well. Terrorism is made use of in another clever policing method that is used to promote racial injustice. For example, while in an area known for its tourism, I observed a group of plainclothes officers assigned to this area randomly stopping individuals and requesting to see their identification. During these encounters, the officers would explain that the location was a highly targeted area for terrorism and they were checking individuals and taking all precautions. The officers would then transmit the subjects' information via radio through the NCIC, checking for warrants while compiling data on these individuals. While continuously observing these officers' interactions with various subjects in this area, I noticed that the subjects were all minorities. White subjects were not stopped as they traveled throughout the area. If you were to examine the numerous radio transmissions by those officers during that period, the information recorded would reveal the disparity of those being stopped and that it was being done arbitrarily. These unlawful stops are tactics used due to an officer's desire to find contraband and check subjects for pending warrants on file when there is no articulable reasonable suspicion of criminal activity. This type of police practice is just one of the many that occurs daily.

Law enforcement policies on the use of *deadly force* vary from agency to agency. Let's talk about the use of *deadly force* as it pertains to police officers and their perception of fear. Is the use of *deadly force* merely a judgment from the perception of the officer versus the actual threat? Following a police shooting, how can one gauge how the officer perceived the actual threat? Was he in fear for his life.

How do we define the *kill zone*? There are many possible explanations. The *kill zone* is the distance of five feet in the area which approximately half of police officers killed during the past ten years were killed in. The closer an offender is to an officer, the greater the opportunity he has to injure or kill that officer. Weapons such as knives and clubs can pose a significant threat to officers at close-proximity. An officer's reaction time also needs to be considered when reacting to such threats. To be prepared and effective in making sound decisions in the *kill zone*, all officers should be well trained in the areas of *deadly force*, particularly at close range. It is equally important for officers to properly access situations that are nonlethal and pose no danger at any given time. The mere fact that someone is in close range to you is not justification for the use of *deadly force*. There are numerous factors that should be considered regarding how officers function in intense situations. An officer's failure to properly process threat levels and other components can result in a violent and even lethal confrontation. Other components may include the officer's cultural awareness, race perception, ability to make split-second decisions under highly charged conditions, response to fear stimulated by other officers, and amount of training in the areas of verbal commands and de-escalation techniques.

Recommendation:

The grand jury should mirror a preliminary hearing. All cases should be conducted in an open hearing on the merits of the case, just like a probable cause hearing. The defendant with his or her attorney will appear and may dispute the prosecutor's charges. The decision will be rendered by a group of citizens brought together to form a grand jury. If the prosecutor's evidence is accepted as factual and sufficient, the suspect is called to stand trial. A special prosecutor should be assigned by the DOJ and is responsible for representing the government in all police related deaths involving others.

The single most deadly trick of the trade is when an officer willfully and purposely uses *deadly force* because of a prevalent misrepresentation of its use. It has been said by senior cops on the streets that if you can justify the shot, then take the shot. Just remember to say the magic words, such as *"I was in fear for my life"* or *"He was reaching for a weapon."* These common phrases are guaranteed to cover you regardless of the situation. Officers believe they can get away with murder if you say one of these two phrases that will exempt you. The incident is exacerbated enormously when officers approach someone without identifying themselves in any way. Another common police practice is when an individual is attempting to flee from police in a vehicle. The subject is in the act of trying to quickly leave the immediate area when the officer steps into the path of the fleeing vehicle and shoots. Police officers believe that no matter what position they're in, they are in extreme danger and can justify *deadly force*. However widespread such an interpretation may be, it is not accurate, and the use of *deadly force* in this fashion is not warranted. A subject attempting to drive away from an officer is not a potentially deadly threat. The officer is aware that the suspect cannot be considered an actual threat justifying *deadly force* until the subject's actions become deadly threatening life. This is when the officer steps into the path of a vehicle attempting to flee and discharges his weapon while claiming to be in fear for his life. The officer knows that so if an individual is not moving or attempting to advance the vehicle, it clearly is not legally justified to use *deadly force* against him or her. Officers who do shoot in those circumstances often find themselves subject to civil litigation and sometimes criminal charges. They are always in violation of their department's standard operating policy in related matters.

Another trick of the trade is how certain situations justify the warrantless search of automobiles on public streets and highways. The police searching automobiles without a warrant has been and always will be an issue of concern for minorities. Does a traffic violation give the police the right to search a vehicle? Is the search limited to the interior of the car, including the glove box and console? The courts have concluded that a warrant-less search of a vehicle is valid if the police have probable cause to believe that the vehicle contains evidence they are attempting to locate. There are several landmark cases such as *Carroll v. United States (1925)* and *United States v. Ross (1982)* where the courts have held that if probable cause exists that a vehicle contains contraband or criminal evidence, a warrantless search by the police is permissible. The most important requirement for a warrantless search of a vehicle is that it must be based on the legal standard of probable cause.

A police officer who searches a vehicle must have reason to believe that it contains evidence of a crime. Under such requirements, the vehicle may be stopped and searched, the contraband seized, and the occupant arrested. Police officers often order minorities out of their vehicles following traffic stops to conduct a pat down to check for weapons while conducting searches of vehicles with the hopes of locating weapons and contraband. Police officers are familiar with the legal ramifications of such stops; they know to use phrases relating to safety. Many traffic stops are conducted by officers with no evidence of suspicious behavior or activity. These types of police acts are conducted routinely while officers continuously circumvent the legal requirements; this promotes governmental invasion of citizens. The courts must focus on two important issues relating to vehicle traffic stops. First, is the stop lawful and a violation of any motor vehicle code? Second, is safety an issue to the officer who orders an individual to exit his vehicle once it is stopped, or is it a typical tool used to search, harass, and inconvenience a motorist who has questioned the validity of the stop? Many traffic stops become simple fishing expeditions in a sea of driving minorities. How many times have you been stopped by the police while driving, or how many people do you know who were stopped, only to hear something false about the nature of the stop? What about those common *phantom stop phrases* such as, "You swerved across the lines in your lane," "You didn't come to a complete stop," "You ran a red light," "You failed to signal," and more? The most famous police phrase used to follow an unwarranted stop is, "You fit the description."

Let's talk about the infamous case of *Pennsylvania v. Mimms (1977).* The U.S. Supreme Court upheld a decision that a police officer ordering a person out of a car following a traffic stop and conducting a pat down to check for weapons did not violate the defendant's Fourth Amendment rights. I will briefly explain the circumstances surrounding this case. Two police officers pulled over a car that had expired license plates. The officers ordered the driver out of the vehicle, at which time an officer noticed a bulge in his pants under his jacket. Following a pat down, the officer discovered a weapon and placed the subject, Harry Mimms, under arrest. He was charged and convicted for carrying a concealed weapon and unlawfully carrying a firearm without a license. The case was reversed by the Pennsylvania Supreme Court, which ruled that the evidence should have been suppressed, as the police violated Mr. Mimms's Fourth Amendment rights. The U.S. Supreme Court reversed the Pennsylvania Supreme Court's decision, upholding the original decision claiming no Fourth

Amendment rights were violated. The state of Pennsylvania believed that the officer had no evidence to be suspicious of Mr. Mimms during the stop as related to his behavior or unusual activity, as nothing was evident during the stop. The state discovered that the officer ordered the drivers to exit their vehicles during all stops. The state defended the officer because he did this to prevent anything from happening to him.

In a six-to-three ruling by the Supreme Court, the decision against Mr. Mimms held that the order to exit the car was reasonable and thus did not violate his Fourth Amendment rights. Justice Thurgood Marshall disagreed and wrote that the frisk the officer conducted could only be permissible under the Fourth Amendment if the search was due to the reason of the stop. The reason that Mr. Mimms was pulled over was due to an expired license plate, which in no way has anything to do with carrying a concealed weapon. He and the other two dissenting justices concluded that the court gave too much leeway in allowing the officers to search Mr. Mimms for any reason.

What do the various sources of police data tell us about police activity in the United States? What is known about police behavior, hate crimes, and crimes against persons by law enforcement? What trends and patterns exist in police related incidents that can help us understand and prevent such cases of police abuse? This information will help us understand the nature of such behavior and plan control methods. For example, if data show that abusive police behavior consistently takes place in low-income areas dominated by minorities, then the abuse may be a function inflicted against a certain segment of the population purposely. If, in contrast, the abuse is spread across the country in various communities, then such abuse may be linked to training.

Recommendation:

A special dash-cam feature installed by auto manufacturers that provides the time and date in high-definition video in the event of an unforeseen incident or accident will make any attorney's case that much stronger. This vehicle camera will be a recorder that captures events in real time as they happen. You as well as law enforcement will be protected in the event of almost anything, such as if your vehicle is stolen and used in a crime like hit and run, carjacking, crimes against an officer's safety, or many other possible situations. The footage that is recording should cover front, rear, left, and right angles to include the interior as well as the exterior. Added special features can allow you to play back video, store incidents on memory cards, and upload immediately for safekeeping. The vehicle camera should be able to locate and retrieve information directly from this special auto-recording software that will automatically sort files by date and time for easy access and viewing.

Finally, I want to talk about a method police officers use to bait individuals into an arrest. There are various kinds of tricks used by law enforcement officers across the country—too many to list. The one sure way to find out about the many different tricks that police officers use is to be around a bunch of cops following gatherings such as training seminars, conferences, parties, or other such activities where they mingle and try to outdo the others with the most insane stories. Fuel the conversation with alcohol and prepare to be amazed at what you hear. One of the most deadly and bizarre stories I've ever heard was an officer explaining how he would create friction within a drug dealer's circle and wait to see deadly consequences because of this dirty tactic. The officer said he would use this setup on drug couriers who disrespected him or caused havoc on his *beat*. This officer said he would surveil his target and wait until the subject was possessing narcotics. He would then jump out on the subject, search him without cause, and recover the drugs. The officer would let the subject go free while placing the drugs into the police property and evidence section, labeling it as found property marked to be destroyed. The officer would get word back to the dealer that the targeted subject was stealing his product from him—an unlawful stop made to create a deadly situation.

I will reveal a couple other examples to stimulate your mind and give you an idea of what road you may be headed down the next time you have some type of police encounter. I recall responding to a domestic call early in my police career. I was assisting a senior officer at this call; the location was a residential community mostly consisting of working-class blacks. The female complainant called the police because her husband was drunk and verbally abusive. I arrived first and began talking with the complainant when the senior officer arrived. We were standing in the foyer area of the house while the husband was upstairs. Moments later, the husband comes down the stairs talking to himself in a loud manner about how he was tired of coming home and feeling unappreciated. The stench of alcohol was wreaking havoc in the air as the husband walked by, at times speaking incoherently. The complainant stated that she just wanted her husband to leave for the night. I explained to her that he was legally in his place of residence and had committed no crime. It was at this moment the senior officer signaled that he was going to step outside momentarily. Shortly thereafter, the senior officer reentered the house and approached the husband. He spoke to him in a very low whisper at a range that no one else could hear. The husband quickly exited the house, and the officer signaled for me to follow him. As we exited the house, the senior officer took out his handcuffs and informed the husband that he was under arrest for being drunk in public. I asked the senior officer, "What the hell just happened?" He replied, "You got to do what you got to do!"

The senior officer explained, "If we didn't take care of this now, we'd be returning to the house a couple more times tonight." I asked him "how did you pull that off." He explained that he went outside and turned on the headlights of the car in the driveway. When he returned, he asked the husband if that was his car in the driveway because the lights were on. It was at that time that the husband quickly left the house to turn off the lights. It was our opportunity to make the move and arrest the husband, make the wife happy, and not return to the house for the rest of the night. Hook, line, and sinker! I've seen officers time and time again pull this move off in several ways. The wife was not happy about her husband being arrested; she just wanted him to leave and go stay at a relative's house.

There are a few other variations to this trick. For example, I've responded to a similar domestic call where officers had no grounds to arrest the aggressor of the dispute, who is usually the male. At this domestic call, the officer went outside the residence and requested a tow truck. The officers told the tow truck driver that the owner may need a tow for his vehicle. The officer instructed the driver to back up and park in front of the vehicle in the driveway and wait momentarily while he located the owner. The officer went back into the house to inform the inebriated male subject that his vehicle was about to be towed relating to some repossession matter. When the subject exited the house, the officer followed behind him to make the drunk in public arrest. The officer then casually walked over to the tow truck driver and told him that the owner of the vehicle changed his mind and that his services would not be needed.

Another slick trick of the trade used to make a quick arrest and get numbers for *comp-stat* is the garbage can shuffle. For this practice, officers will go to a nearby park where signs are posted that prohibit trespassing during specified hours. As soon as the park closes, officers will go directly to the park entrances and pathways near the outer sidewalks. They will then relocate trash cans several feet away from the sidewalk outside of the park to within the park along the walkways. Officers will then wait, lurking in the shadows, for someone to walk by and discard something into a trash can. Once this occurs, the officers will jump out of their hidden places to charge the individual with trespassing in the park after hours.

One of the most notorious arrests using the "coax him out of the door to jail" trick was the case involving Henry Louis Gates Jr., who was charged with disorderly conduct on the grounds of Harvard University. A copy of the police report stated that on July 16, 2009, Mr. Gates was placed under arrest after being observed exhibiting loud and tumultuous behavior in a public place directed at a uniformed police officer who was investigating a crime in progress. It was at this point that Sergeant Crowley became a fisherman and made the big catch. Listen to Sergeant Crowley's statement from the report: "As I began walking through the foyer toward the front door, I could hear Gates demanding my name. I told Gates that I would speak with him outside. My reason for wanting to leave the residence was that Gates was yelling very loud and the acoustics of the kitchen and foyer were making it difficult for me to transmit pertinent information to the Emergency Communications Center (ECC) or other responding units." Once Mr. Gates exited his residence, he was arrested with the *catch-all offense* of disorderly conduct, which restricts the use of certain vocal behavior in public. I'm certain the arresting officer described Mr. Gates's behavior using words and phrases that were in some form abusive, profane, and communicated in a loud and vulgar manner, making this a hostile act in the presence of others in a public place. If Mr. Gates had knowledge of how police officers use such laws, he would have remained in his dwelling and avoided one of the oldest tricks of the trade.

Attached is a copy of the incident report involving Mr. Gates's arrest. One can only imagine if bodycam footage were available during this incident, there would be no doubt as to the exaggerated sequence of events written in the officer's report in comparison to the actual incident that was recorded.

CAMBRIDGE POLICE DEPARTMENT
CAMBRIDGE, MA

Incident Report #9005127
Report Entered: 07/16/2009 13:21:34

Case Title	Location	Apt/Unit #
	◆ WARE ST	

Date/Time Reported
07/16/2009 12:44:00

Date/Time Occurred
to

Incident Type/Offense
1.) DISORDERLY CONDUCT c272 S53 —

Reporting Officer
CROWLEY, JAMES (467)

Approving Officer
WILSON III, JOSEPH (213)

Persons

Role	Name	Sex Race Age DOB	Phone	Address
WITNESS	WHALEN, LUCIA	40	H ▬▬▬ C ▬▬▬ MA	▬▬▬▬▬▬

Offenders

Status	Name	Sex	Race	Age DOB	Phone	Address
DEFENDANT	GATES, HENRY	MALE	BLACK	58 - ▬▬▬	H ▬▬▬ C	◆ WARE ST CAMBRIDGE, MA

Vehicles

Property

Class	Description	Make	Model	Serial #	Value

Narrative

On Thursday July 16, 2009, Henry Gates, Jr. ▬▬▬▬ of ◆ Ware Street, Cambridge, MA) was placed under arrest at ◆ Ware Street, after being observed exhibiting loud and tumultuous behavior, in a public place, directed at a uniformed police officer who was present investigating a report of a crime in progress. These actions on the behalf of Gates served no legitimate purpose and caused citizens passing by this location to stop and take notice while appearing surprised and alarmed.

On the above time and date, I was on uniformed duty in an unmarked police cruiser assigned to the Administration Section, working from 7:00 AM-3:30 PM. At approximately 12:44 PM, I was operating my cruiser on Harvard Street near Ware Street. At that time, I overheard an ECC broadcast for a possible break in progress at ◆ Ware Street. Due to my proximity, I responded.

When I arrived at ◆ Ware Street I radioed ECC and asked that they have the caller meet me at the front door to this residence. I was told that the caller was already outside. As I was getting this information, I climbed the porch stairs toward the front door. As I reached the door, a female voice called out to me. I turned and looked in the direction of the voice and observed a white female, later identified as Lucia Whalen. Whalen, who was standing on the sidewalk in front of the residence, held a wireless telephone in her hand and told me that it was she who called. She went on to tell me that she observed what appeared to be two black males with backpacks on the porch of ◆ Ware Street. She told me that her suspicions were aroused when she observed one of the men wedging his shoulder into the door as if he was trying to force entry. Since I was the only police officer on location and had my back to the front door as I spoke with her, I asked that she wait for other responding officers while I investigated further.

143

As I turned and faced the door, I could see an older black male standing in the foyer of ⬤ Ware Street. I made this observation through the glass paned front door. As I stood in plain view of this man, later identified as Gates, I asked if he would step out onto the porch and speak with me. He replied "no I will not". He then demanded to know who I was. I told him that I was "Sgt. Crowley from the Cambridge Police" and that I was "investigating a report of a break in progress" at the residence. While I was making this statement, Gates opened the front door and exclaimed "why, because I'm a black man in America?". I then asked Gates if there was anyone else in the residence. While yelling, he told me that it was none of my business and accused me of being a racist police officer. I assured Gates that I was responding to a citizen's call to the Cambridge Police and that the caller was outside as we spoke. Gates seemed to ignore me and picked up a cordless telephone and dialed an unknown telephone number. As he did so, I radioed on channel 1 that I was off in the residence with someone who appeared to be a resident but very uncooperative. I then overheard Gates asking the person on the other end of his telephone call to "get the chief" and "what's the chief's name?". Gates was telling the person on the other end of the call that he was dealing with a racist police officer in his home. Gates then turned to me and told me that I had no idea who I was "messing" with and that I had not heard the last of it. While I was led to believe that Gates was lawfully in the residence, I was quite surprised and confused with the behavior he exhibited toward me. I asked Gates to provide me with photo identification so that I could verify that he resided at ⬤ Ware Street and so that I could radio my findings to ECC. Gates initially refused, demanding that I show him identification but then did supply me with a Harvard University identification card. Upon learning that Gates was affiliated with Harvard, I radioed and requested the presence of the Harvard University Police.

With the Harvard University identification in hand, I radioed my findings to ECC on channel two and prepared to leave. Gates again asked for my name which I began to provide. Gates began to yell over my spoken words by accusing me of being a racist police officer and leveling threats that he wasn't someone to mess with. At some point during this exchange, I became aware that Off. Carlos Figueroa was standing behind me. When Gates asked a third time for my name, I explained to him that I had provided it at his request two separate times. Gates continued to yell at me. I told Gates that I was leaving his residence and that if he had any other questions regarding the matter, I would speak with him outside of the residence.

As I began walking through the foyer toward the front door, I could hear Gates again demanding my name. I again told Gates that I would speak with him outside. My reason for wanting to leave the residence was that Gates was yelling very loud and the acoustics of the kitchen and foyer were making it difficult for me to transmit pertinent information to ECC or other responding units. His reply was "ya, I'll speak with your mama outside". When I left the residence, I noted that there were several Cambridge and Harvard University police officers assembled on the sidewalk in front of the residence. Additionally, the caller, Ms. Walen and at least seven unidentified passers-by were looking in the direction of Gates, who had followed me outside of the residence.

As I descended the stairs to the sidewalk, Gates continued to yell at me, accusing me of racial bias and continued to tell me that I had not heard the last of him. Due to the tumultuous manner Gates had exhibited in his residence as well as his continued tumultuous behavior outside the residence, in view of the public, I warned Gates that he was becoming disorderly. Gates ignored my warning and continued to yell, which drew the attention of both the police officers and citizens, who appeared surprised and alarmed by Gates's outburst. For a second time I warned Gates to calm down while I withdrew my department issued handcuffs from their carrying case. Gates again ignored my warning and continued to yell at me. It was at this time that I informed Gates that he was under arrest. I then stepped up the stairs, onto the porch and attempted to place handcuffs on Gates. Gates initially resisted my attempt to handcuff him, yelling that he was "disabled" and would fall without his cane. After the handcuffs were properly applied, Gates complained that they were too tight. I ordered Off. Ivey, who was among the responding officers, to handcuff Gates with his arms in front of him for his comfort while I secured a cane for Gates from within the residence. I then asked Gates if he would like an officer to take possession of his house key and secure his front door, which he left wide open. Gates told me that the door was un securable due to a previous break attempt at the residence. Shortly thereafter, a Harvard University maintenance person arrived on scene and appeared familiar with Gates. I asked Gates if he was comfortable with this Harvard University maintenance person securing his residence. He told me that he was.

After a brief consultation with Sgt. Lashley and upon Gates's request, he was transported to 125 6th. Street in a police cruiser (Car 1, Off's Graham and Ivey) where he was booked and processed by Off. J. P. Crowley.

THE U.S. CONSTITUTION

Amendment I [1791]
Congress shall make no law respecting an establish-ment of religion or prohibiting the free exercise thereof; or abridging the freedom of speech, or of the press; or the right of the people to peaceably assembly, and to petition the government for a redress of grievances.

Amendment II [1791]
A well-regulated Militia, being necessary to the security of a free State, the right of the people to keep and bear Arms, shall not be infringed.

Amendment III [1791]
No Soldier shall, in time of peace be quartered in any house, without the consent of the Owner, nor in time of war, but in a manner to be prescribed by law.

Amendment IV [1791]
The right of the people to be secure in their persons, houses, papers, and effects, against unreasonable searches and seizure, shall not be violated, and no Warrants shall issue, but upon probable cause, supported by Oath or affirmation, and particularly describing the place to be searched, and the persons or things to be seized.

Amendment V [1791]
No person shall be held to answer for a capital, or otherwise infamous crime, unless on a presentment or indictment

of a Grand Jury, except in cases arising in the land or naval forces, or in the Militia, when in actual service in time of War or public danger; nor shall any person be subject for the same offence to be twice put in jeopardy of life or limb; nor shall be compelled in any criminal case to be a witness against himself, nor be deprived of life, liberty, or property, without due process of law; nor shall private property be taken for public use, without just compensation.

Amendment VI [1791]
In all criminal prosecutions, the accused shall enjoy the right to a speedy and public trial, by an impartial jury of the State and district wherein the crime shall have been committed, which district shall have been previously ascertained by law, and to be informed of the nature and cause of the accusations; to be confronted with the witnesses against him; to have compulsory process for obtaining witnesses in his favor, and to have the Assistance of Counsel for his defense.

Amendment VII [1791]
In suits at common law, where the value in controversy shall exceed twenty dollars, the right of trial by jury shall be preserved, and no fact tried by jury, shall be otherwise re-examined in any Court of the United States, then according to the rules of the common law.

Amendment VIII [1791]
Excessive bail shall not be required, nor excessive fines imposed, nor cruel and unusual punishments inflicted.

Amendment IX [1791]

The enumeration in the Constitution, of certain rights, shall not be construed to deny or disparage others retained by the people.

Amendment X [1791]

The powers not delegated to the United States by the Constitution, nor prohibited by it to the States, are reserved to the States respectively, or to the people.

Amendment XI [1798]

The judicial power of the United States shall not be construed to extend to any suit in law or equity, commenced or prosecuted against one of the United States by Citizens of another State, or by Citizens or Subjects of any Foreign State.

Amendment XII [1804]

The Electors shall meet in their respective states, and vote by ballot for President and Vice-President, one of whom, at least, shall not be an inhabitant of the same state with themselves; they shall name in their ballots the person voted for President, and in distinct ballots the person voted for as Vice-President, and they shall make distinct lists of all persons voted for as President, and of all persons voted for as Vice-President, and of the number of votes for each, which lists they shall sign and certify, and transmit sealed to the seat of the government of the United States, directed to the President of the Senate. The President of the Senate shall, in the presence of the Senate and House of Representatives, open all the certificates and the votes shall then be counted. The person having the greatest number of votes for President, shall be the President, if such number be a majority of the whole number of Electors appointed; and if no person have such majority, then from the persons having the highest numbers not exceeding three on the list of those voted for as President, the House of Representatives shall choose immediately, by ballot, the President. But in choosing the President, the votes shall be taken by states, the representation from each state having one vote; a quorum for this purpose shall consist of a member or members from two-thirds of the states, and most of all states shall be necessary to a choice. And if the House of Representatives shall not choose a President whenever the right of choice shall devolve upon them, before the fourth day of March next following, then the Vice President shall act as President, as in the case of the death or other constitutional disability of the President. The person having the greatest number of votes as Vice President, shall be the Vice President, if such number be a majority of the whole number of Electors appointed, and if no person have a majority, then from the two highest numbers on the list, the Senate shall choose the Vice-President; a quorum for the purpose shall consist of two-thirds of the whole number of Senators, and a majority of the whole number shall be necessary to a choice. But no person constitutionally ineligible to the office of President shall be eligible to that of Vice-President of the United States.

Amendment XIII [1865]
Section 1: Neither slavery nor involuntary servitude, except as a punishment for crime whereof the party shall have been duly convicted, shall exist within the United States, or any place subject to their jurisdiction.

Section 2 Congress shall have power to enforce this article by appropriate legislation.

Amendment XIV [1868]
Section 1: All persons born or naturalized in the United States, and subject to the jurisdiction thereof, are citizens of the United States and of the State wherein they reside. No State shall make or enforce any law which shall abridge the privileges or immunities of citizens of the United States; nor shall any State deprive any person of life, liberty, or property, without due process of law; nor deny to any person within its jurisdiction the equal protection of the laws.

Section 2: Representatives shall be apportioned among the several States according to their respective numbers, counting the whole number of persons in each State, excluding Indians not taxed. But when the right to vote at any election for the choice of electors for President and Vice President of the United States, Representatives in Congress, the Executive and Judicial officers of a State, or the members of the Legislature thereof, is denied to any of the male inhabitants of such State, being twenty-one years of age, and citizens of the United States, or in any way abridged, except for participation in rebellion, or other crime, the basis of representation therein shall be reduced in the proportion which the number of such male citizens shall bear to the whole number of male citizens twenty-one years of age in such State.

Section 3: No person shall be a Senator or Representative in Congress, or elector of President and Vice President, or hold any office, civil or military, under the United States, or under any State, who having previously taken an oath, as a member of Congress, or as an officer of the United States, or as a member of any State Legislature, or as an executive or judicial officer of any State, to support the Constitution of the United States, shall have engaged in insurrection or rebellion against the same, or given aid or comfort to the enemies thereof. But Congress may by a vote of two-thirds of each House, remove such disability.

Section 4: The validity of the public debt of the United States, authorized by law, including debts incurred for payment of pensions and bounties for services in suppressing insurrection or rebellion, shall not be questioned. But neither the United States nor any State shall assume or pay any debt or obligation incurred in aid of insurrection or rebellion against the United States, or any claim for the loss or emancipation of any slave; but all such debts, obligations and claims shall be held illegal and void.

Section 5: The Congress shall have power to enforce, by appropriate legislation, the provisions of this article.

Amendment XV [1870]

Section 1: The right of citizens of the United States to vote shall not be denied or abridged by the United States or by any State because of race, color, or previous condition of servitude.

Section 2: The Congress shall have the power to enforce this article by appropriate legislation.

ABOUT THE AUTHOR

Author Joseph Ested grew up in a poor neighborhood in Brooklyn, New York. Joe came from a broken home without his mother or father. He spent most of his childhood in the foster care system. But that did not stop him from pursuing a career in law enforcement. He has held positions in law enforcement as a police officer, police Investigator, sheriff's deputy, and a corrections officer working directly with inmates. He held a security clearance with the Department of State and Department of Homeland Security.

Later in his career, Ested served in Afghanistan as a police advisor and police instructor for the Afghanistan Police Training Program. He was then elected to vice president for the Police Union. Joe has been awarded numerous honors for his contributions to the law enforcement community. He is currently a Department of Criminal Justice instructor.

ACKNOWLEDGEMENT

I would like to thank my brother, Anthony Ested, who was instrumental in the creation and completion of this book. He exemplified commitment and support during this journey. His knowledge in law enforcement and the criminal justice system was essential.

ENDNOTES/CREDITS

Chapter 3 – Discretion or Discrimination

1. New York Civil Liberties Union (NYCLU) – Stop & Frisk Statistical Data, pg. 36-37.
2. New York Daily News, 2017, p. 37. The City of New York has agreed to pay up to $75 million in a class-action lawsuit settlement involving the NYPD's reckless behavior.

Chapter 6 – The Cover-Up

1. Daily News article, *"Cover- Up"* (2014). An NYPD internal report was prepared following the death of Eric Garner that downplayed the seriousness of his conditions after the incident, pg. 96.
2. (S210.00 Perjury and Related Offenses), pg. 103-104.
3. Cleveland Police Department (Use of Force Policy), March 1, 2002 (effective date), August 8, 2014 (revised date), pgs. 105-119.

Chapter 7 – Tricks of the Trade

1. Fourth Amendment of the U.S. Constitution, pg. 121.
2. NYS Criminal Procedure Law (S140.50 Temporary Questioning of persons in public places; search for weapons), pg. 123-124.
3. NYPD Form PD 383-153 (06-15) (What is a stop card?), pg. 125.

4. *Terry v. Ohio (1968).* The NYS criminal procedure law authorizes the *stop-and-frisk* procedure using standards established by the Supreme Court. Police officers are lawfully allowed to stop, question, and frisk subjects while investigating suspicious behavior without having to meet any probable cause standards, pg. 126.

5. *Carroll v. United States (1925)* and *United States v. Ross (1982).* The courts have held that *if probable cause exists* that a vehicle contains contraband or criminal evidence, a warrantless search by the police is permissible, pg. 134.

6. *Pennsylvania v. Mimms (1977).* The U.S. Supreme Court upheld a decision that a police officer ordering a person out of a car following a traffic stop and conducting a pat down to check for weapons did not violate the defendant's Fourth Amendment rights, pg. 135-136.

7. Cambridge Police Department - Incident Report #9005127, July 16, 2009, (Re: Henry L. Gates, Jr. Arrest), pg. 143-144.

United States Constitution, pgs. 145-151.

GLOSSARY

aggressive behavioral approach – police officer tends to be irritable, impulsive, coercive, and condescending.

beat – a geographical area that a police officer patrols.

blue wall of silence – the hidden and protected culture that isolates policing from the rest of society.

broken windows theory – visible signs of crime or disorder within a community when left untreated encourages additional crime and disorder.

catch-all offense – justification used by police personnel that allows an arrest when no other justification is warranted, e.g. the suspect was disorderly and resisting.

catch-all phrases – statements used by police personnel to justify use of force while avoiding accounttability, e.g. *"in fear of my life/he's reaching for a weapon."*

chokehold – a technique that involves applying pressure around a person's neck to restrain them while restricting them from breathing.

comp-stat system – short for compare statistics is a system used to identify and combat crime while creating quality of life improvements. The system identifies increases in crime through the usage of comparative statistics throughout various geographical areas.

criminal subculture – a separate group that is part of the dominant culture that created and maintains a unique set of social/criminal disorganized traditions, beliefs, and values.

deadly force – the authority of law enforcement to kill individuals who they presume are resisting arrest or present a danger to the officer or the community.

departmentalized – when a police officer conforms to and becomes established in the practices and customs of police culture; affecting their performance, behavior, and identity.

excessive force – the amount of force which is used that is greater than what a reasonable, and prudent; law enforcement officer would use under the circumstances present.

good ol' boy system – a selective group of white males particularly in the southern states who control majority of law enforcement agencies solely to influence personnel related matters.

kill zone – an area in which an approaching adversary can be trapped, ambushed, and/or killed.

methodical behavioral approach – detects, screens, and processes information relating to potential criminal offenders.

phantom stop phrases – a method that is factitious in nature, giving police a reason to stop you legally; e.g. I'm stopping you because you fit the description.

plain clothes officers – law enforcement personnel that is dressed in ordinary clothes.

police culture – an occupational culture that becomes socialized by unorthodox and illegal methods of socialization that shapes routine decision-making.

police culture traits – personality traits typically can be described as authoritarian, suspicious, racist, violent, hostile, and insecure.

police quotas – an established system used by police management to predetermine a specified number of arrest an officer must provide within a given time frame.

protective sweeps – to allow officers to conduct a limited search of the suspect, belongings, and surrounding area to ensure their safety.

tactical positioning – to maintain a safe distance from potential danger and to allow sufficient reaction time in the event of an attack.

street training – the radical, illegal unorthodox methods used compared to conventional methods learned during standard training.

stop-encounter card – a document used by law enforcement officers to record when, where, and why contact with an individual who police suspect may have committed a criminal act is made.

stop-and-frisk – encounters when police approach individuals who they think are acting suspicious. Officers will run their hands over the subject's clothing attempting to locate weapons.

unwritten code – to stick up for each other against all others, and not to rat each other out.

use of force – the amount of force used by police that is deemed necessary to gain control of a subject. The amount of force used should be comparable to the amount of resistance.

work slowdown – deliberate acts by police personnel to reduce the rate of work productivity in the police department.